SHADOW SOLDIERS

OF THE

AMERICAN REVOLUTION

LOYALIST TALES *from*
NEW YORK *to* CANADA

MARK JODOIN

Charleston — London

THE
History
PRESS

Published by The History Press
Charleston, SC 29403
www.historypress.net

Copyright © 2009 by Mark Jodoin
All rights reserved

First published 2009

Manufactured in the United States

ISBN 978.1.59629.726.5

Library of Congress CIP data applied for.

For Harold, David and Brian:
three guys who knew how to tell a story.

CONTENTS

FOREWORD

If there was one thing I discovered during the three and a half years I was privileged to serve my country in Canada, it was this: most Canadians think they know *everything* about America, and most Americans think they know *enough* about Canada. The truth is, Americans and Canadians alike would be well served to know and understand one another a lot better. This book is one wonderful way to bridge that learning gap.

I served as the United States ambassador to Canada during a pivotal time in history for our two great democracies. In a post-9/11 world, our nations' heroes stood shoulder to shoulder fighting terrorists in Afghanistan; we worked to protect and enhance our trade relationship (the world's largest and most productive); and we confronted daunting economic challenges.

The work was supremely rewarding. Canadians are dynamic, generous people who made me and my wife, Susan, always feel at home. Their generosity (and in the case of the Vancouver Rescue Squad, their bravery) in the wake of Hurricane Katrina is etched on our hearts forever.

This is the essence of the American-Canadian bond. Regretfully, however, the demands of modern-day cynicism and politics cause many of our citizens to reflect more on the negative than on our long and positive shared history, which precedes the American War of Independence of the 1770s and '80s.

As a boy growing up in South Carolina, I learned how the American victory over the British in the Revolutionary War led to the expulsion and exile of many Tories who remained loyal to England and King George III. Many of these British-American Loyalists left for Canada, the Bahamas or other nearby outposts of England.

As ambassador to Canada, I had the privilege of living in the beautiful city of Ottawa, which is less than an hour's drive from the New York border. There is rich history in and around this area. Veterans of the Revolutionary War opened up what soon became Upper Canada—an eighteenth-century frontier inhabited by Canada's First Peoples. Known as Ontario since Canada's Confederation in 1867, it is the country's most populous province.

This book is all about the original ties that bind our two nations. You'll read about Ira Honeywell—the first settler on the Ottawa River—and about his father, Sergeant Rice Honeywell, who served as an officer in the United States Continental army and saw much action during several significant battles in New York during the Revolutionary War. He fell in love with the daughter of a Loyalist and spy and followed her and her family to Canada at the end of the Revolutionary War. After a brief spell in a Kingston prison on suspicion of being an American sympathizer (which he was), he went on to marry and become a successful entrepreneur and land speculator on the Canadian shore of the St. Lawrence River.

Colonel Joel Stone was a Connecticut Yankee who spent much of the war fighting for the British on Long Island and in New York. Stone survived stints in Patriot prisons, being wounded in battle and being shipwrecked in Long Island Sound as he made his way north to settle the pretty town of Gananoque, the gateway to the Thousand Islands and the annual summer playground to thousands of Canadian and American tourists and vacationers.

There are many more such stories contained in Mark Jodoin's *Shadow Soldiers of the American Revolution: Loyalist Tales from New York to Canada*. Mr. Jodoin casts light on many British Americans who fought with valor and honor equal to American Patriots but have remained, for many, in the shadows of North American history.

I write this as a South Carolinian devoted to the American-Canadian relationship, and I take great pleasure in the fact that this book will be brought to market by a South Carolina publisher. My country has long been blessed by Canada's friendship. This is a partnership that has stood the test of time. Mark Jodoin's fine work of heritage writing helps us better understand our shared histories. I hope it leads us to better appreciate our shared stake in tomorrow.

David Wilkins
U.S. Ambassador to Canada, 2005–09
Greenville, South Carolina
April 2009

AUTHOR'S NOTE

Most Canadian readers will notice my use of American spelling. Canadian English generally follows British spelling, though American alternatives can be occasionally used. As this book has been printed and brought to market by a publisher in the United States, it is appropriate that American spelling be employed throughout.

The images contained in this book are copyright free unless otherwise noted. My use of prints by the prolific British illustrator W.H. Barlett may seem unusual in that they were drawn early in the nineteenth century; his are not unlike those created by later U.S. historian Benson J. Lossing with which Americans are likely to be more familiar. My intention was to introduce Bartlett's iconic Canadian images to American audiences whenever possible.

My sketches are based on site visits or photographs and provided when no image or illustration was available or practical. In situations whereby no known image exists, I have provided an interpretation based on the vernacular of the day.

Lastly, I am responsible for the maps, and any mistakes in geographic positioning or chronology are mine.

ACKNOWLEDGEMENTS

The difference between a heritage writer and a historian was made indelibly clear to me under the most pleasant of circumstances in the summer of 2008.

I received a letter in response to a history feature I had written for the monthly magazine *Esprit de Corps*, the factual yet opinionated staple of Canada's military and defense communities. The envelope's return name was instantly recognizable to me: Mary Beacock Fryer UE. As I unfolded her letter, my mind regressed to the excitement and unease of a student about to be graded.

Ms. Fryer's name carries historical heft. Her prolific and decades-long career could fill a library on its own. The breadth and depth of her work on the colonial history of Ontario is remarkable: biographies of frontier spies and Loyalists, commemorations and institutional histories and that trickiest genre of all, historical fiction written with a factual foundation. Her letter to me was courteous, charming and of course contained a helpful correction.

That piece of correspondence led to a lunch invitation to join her and her husband at their cottage on the St. Lawrence River near Brockville, Ontario. Their summer home sits on the edge of a bay, and on that calm July day, her husband, a historian of note in his own right, kindly allowed me and Mary to indulge and chat as two colonial history fanatics might. In truth, the conversation was unidirectional—I put my longstanding curiosities to her while she, in turn, relieved me of the burden of unawareness.

"How torn must Sir John Johnson have been in early 1777?" I asked. He was forced, after all, to leave his cherished family and beloved home in New York and escape to Canada to elude the impending grasp of Continental army general Elias Dayton. "How could British spy Dr. George Smyth manage to operate for so long, literally and figuratively, in a crowded rebel hospital in Albany?" He continued to do so after having been caught, imprisoned and released on a previous occasion.

As our conversation progressed, it was clear that Mary's replies were detailed beyond any that one might expect from a senior in her retirement years, long removed from her studies at the University of Toronto and Edinburgh University. Her knowledge was that of a true historian, assembled through long, arduous hours in silent archives, acquired by a mind as remarkable as the topics on which she wrote.

I returned to Ottawa with the realization that the role of a heritage writer was utterly dependent on the forbearance and perseverance of historians such as Mary Fryer. To her and others like her, I am indebted.

Though I regret that we have not met as yet, doubtless a conversation with Gavin Watt or Timothy Compeau would have the same tenor, albeit on different topics. The former is a longstanding Loyalist historian of excellent reputation whose work with James Morrison has documented the burning of the Mohawk Valley and the activities of Sir John Johnson and Captain John Deserontyon, among others. The latter is an emerging historian whose revealing studies of the enigmatic Colonel Joel Stone have honored the city of Gananoque and enlightened many others, including me.

Also appreciated is the work of Elizabeth Hoople, who so clearly applied her heart as much as her mind to the story of the heroic family from which she is descended. This applies equally to Parks Honeywell and his editing of Doris May Honeywell's drafts of biographical reference recounting the exploits of American Rice Honeywell and his son Ira, the first settler in Canada's capital of Ottawa.

Sue Bazely and the volunteers at the Cataraqui Archaeological Research Foundation have contributed much to the historical record of the Kingston area with their—pardon the pun—groundbreaking work on Mary Brant. I have also drawn upon the many works of Glenn Lockwood, who adds yearly to his status as the definitive historian of eastern Ontario. His accounts of the Smyth family and all others who helped populate this region have helped popularize it as well.

From other high-profile historians such as former Saskatchewan cabinet minister Janice Potter McKinnon, who wrote of the ordeals of Loyalist women and their families, to the unsung graduate students who are at this moment gently holding historical documents up to the light of scrutiny, I offer my thanks.

I offer them, too, to my friend and mentor Coral Lindsay, who, like all instinctive teachers, knows when to drop one slipper so that her student will pursue the other. Coral, along with my friend Georgina Tupper and others, is a founder and member of the Rideau Township Historical Society (RTHS), a dedicated group of heritage enthusiasts for whom I am honored to serve as president. To the other members of the RTHS executive—Jane Anderson, Owen Cooke, Jeff Cronin, Brian Earl, Brian Killins, Lucy Martin, Susan McKellar and Ron Wilson—I offer my thanks for their patience with my many absences and oversights. And thanks to many good friends of the RTHS such as Cameron Trueman, whose knack for connecting historical dots for young people is heartening, and to City of Ottawa politician Glenn Brooks, who, despite a list of priorities as long as a council meeting, finds time to support the RTHS, its mission and its heritage programs.

More recent friends have been helpful too. Adelaide Lanktree and her sister Louise Hall of the Sir John Johnson Branch of the United Empire Loyalist Association of Canada (UELAC) have yet to deny me a favor, no matter how obscure. They have introduced me to other helpful members of UELAC, such as Michel Racicot, branch president Rod Riordon, president of the association's Heritage Branch Robert Wilkins and the national president of the association, Mr. Frederick H. Hayward UE. Fred has encouraged me from the moment we shook hands on a snowy winter's night in Montreal.

A Canadian government friend of note is Gavin Liddy, who by happenstance is my neighbor in addition to being the former superintendent of Parks Canada's Rideau Canal. While he read my stories with enthusiasm and encouragement, he assisted his colleague Pam Buell, who led a team to a remarkable coup de grâce: ensuring that the Rideau Canal assumed its rightful place among other UNESCO World Heritage Sites.

American friends, old and new, have proved invaluable too. Caryn Mathes's instincts were beyond helpful, and Matt Puccini and Dave Carlen are true red, white and blue American entrepreneurs. Christy Cox and Ashley Martin from Columbia, South Carolina, supported Ambassador David Wilkins through seemingly endless Ottawa winters. They have returned to their more agreeable climate and remain the embodiment of southern charm. During his recent term as United States ambassador to Canada, Ambassador Wilkins acquitted himself with much honor to the benefit of both Americans and Canadians, using his astute, subtle and at times not-so-subtle diplomacy. It is a privilege to have his foreword as the first words in this modest book.

On the publishing side, thanks to Hannah Cassilly of The History Press for patiently listening to my pitch in the foyer of the Washington, D.C. Historical Society and to her highly competent colleague, commissioning editor Kate Pluhar, who by now is convinced that the Canadian calendar is set weeks, more likely months, behind the American calendar. Jaime Muehl, a loyal if not Loyalist New Yorker, edited my text as only a devout follower of Chicago style could. Closer to home, thanks to Scott and Kathy Taylor, the two forces of nature behind *Esprit de Corps* magazine, and to their benign and forgiving publisher, Jules Simone, and their less forgiving but equally agreeable editor, Darcy Knoll.

I appreciate the interest of friends such as Nathan Rudyk, John Nyhuus, Pam Faulkner, Chris Johnson, John Flood, Paul Kitchen, Jan Hughes, Marc Leduc and Claudia Currie, who looked in on my concussed health, writing habits and the ups and downs in between. I appreciate my siblings, Peg, Steve and Chris, and my mother, Helen, for not rolling their eyes at my excitement over events that originated in another country two and a quarter centuries ago. Thanks to my friend and neighbor Shelly Kovacs for her equanimity of appraisal and for making dog walks about more than the musings of history. Thanks to my dearest of friends Kelly Hunter, who provided great company and even better photographs while helping me safely navigate the back roads of New York and Vermont. Lastly, thanks to the well-read Maxwell and Floyd for their unwavering support.

As is the case with all first-time authors, my acknowledgements have been lengthy, and rightly so. However, I cannot close without thanking the driver of the car that destroyed mine—and nearly me—one rainy April day in the recent past. My period of recovery provided me the time to read, research and write the material contained herein. May any enjoyment derived from this book proceed like his driving: with reckless abandon and feckless speed.

INTRODUCTION

The term "shadow soldiers" is usually applied to the twenty-first-century dogs of war, the mercenaries of all races who supplement enlisted military troops with tactics frequently exceeding the rules of engagement. These men—for mercenaries are almost universally men—rarely appear on any formal list of combatants. Theirs is an ambiguous, shadowy presence in such places as Africa, Asia and the Middle East.

The term as applied to these pages carries a much different meaning. In eighteenth-century North America, shadow soldiers were far from hidden, were rarely ambiguous, were of the white, Native American and black races and counted women among their numbers. They appeared on the muster rolls of New England militia and provincial units such as the King's Loyal Rangers of New York. Condemned as Tories, Royalists or as King's Men in America, they were lauded as Loyalists in Canada and Britain. Most important, shadow soldiers of the late 1700s fed their loyalties with tenacity while their modern-day namesakes would sell theirs for a bowl of soup.

The crime of shadow soldiers in the 1770s was one of judgment: they supported the losing side in the Revolutionary War. Loyalty to Britain cost them their reputations, homes and country through no fault of their own. The British replied to the resolve of the rebels with inadequate command and wanting tactics. In the centuries since this epic defeat, loyal British Americans have languished in the shadows of continental history, albeit much less so in Canada than in the United States.

North of the border, Loyalists are correctly recalled as nation builders; south of the border, they are the unremembered. Their disloyalty to the Patriot cause has left only rare signs of commemoration—and more often than not, their traceability has been made deliberately demanding. From

New York to New Orleans and cities along the way, statues of Loyalists are few.

One exception is Johnstown, New York, where British-American Sir William Johnson, the first man deemed worthy of a baronetcy in the New World, stands boldly cast in bronze. He oversaw the Mohawks, their valley and the winding river that bears their tribal name. An Irishman by birth, he was an accomplished New Yorker and the most highly regarded white figure in the history of northern natives. He was a builder of America in the mid-eighteenth century long before nation building became fashionable in America.

After his death on the eve of the Revolution, the Patriots of the province of New York desecrated his grave and forced fearful Loyalists to flee north to the Canadian border. Chief among those fleeing was his son, Sir John Johnson, who soon returned as paladin to the defiant young soldiers, spies and scouts who marched alongside him. They fought to regain their homes and farms in the Mohawk, Champlain and Hudson Valleys but were eventually defeated and banished from their New York homelands forever.

Some flourished in Canada as they had in America; others suffered despair and destitution, but most pined for friends and families left behind. All were proud New Yorkers before the American Revolution intervened and changed their lives forever.

Many of their families had, over several generations, helped build America's largest colony, New York. Forced into northern exile, they contributed to three of Canada's future provinces, Ontario, Quebec and Nova Scotia. In the case of southern Ontario, their new homes were carved out of Quebec's western flank and offered as additional recompense for their military service. For noncombatants, simply being loyal was enough to acquire land in lesser amounts.

They and their descendants opened up Canada west of the Ottawa River, where the long reach of Sir William Johnson can be found to this day as it is throughout these pages. He was a seminal figure in the lives of Captain Joseph Brant and his sister, Mary, more commonly known as Molly. Johnson was a mentor to his son and successor, John, and was an inspirational figure for the game and courageous Captain John Deserontyon. Not by coincidence, three of these four are of the Mohawk people, who reluctantly traded the rivers and lakes of north and western New York for the St. Lawrence River and the north and westerly shores of Lake Ontario.

By contrast, the story of Sergeant Rice Honeywell of General George Washington's Continental army also appears here, not for reasons of war but for those of love. Honeywell fought in several major battles of the

Revolutionary War, after which his love for the daughter of a Tory spy led him north. He joined her and her family in Prescott in Canada, across the St. Lawrence from Ogdensburg, New York. Before long he was locked behind the doors of a Canadian prison on grounds that he was an American sympathizer, an accusation that held some truth. Once released, he and his family prospered, and his son went on to become the first pioneer of Ottawa, the eventual capital of his new country.

The dualities within British army captain Joseph Brant are also told here. New York might have remained homeland to the infamous Iroquois leader from New York's Mohawk Valley had the British won the Revolutionary War. A compelling statesman, he was an equally competent warrior but eventually had to settle his Mohawk people in Canada along the Grand River on the western tip of Lake Ontario. Ironically, he later became an advisor to President George Washington on matters relating to the Indians of the American northwest.

New York offered Mary Hoople heartbreak and hope and provided geographic bookends for her long and remarkable life. Her family was murdered and scattered in a brutal Delaware raid in 1780, and she and her younger brother were taken prisoner. Rescued years later by a British officer, she had lost her birth language, culture and knowledge of her only surviving relatives. Fate brought her to the north shore of the St. Lawrence River, west of Cornwall across from Massena, New York, where she was reunited with her only surviving sibling seventy years after their abduction and separation. Having been raised a native medicine woman she received an honorarium and commendation from U.S. president James Madison for her traditional healing of an American soldier during the War of 1812.

Major Edward Jessup and his brother Ebenezer were businessmen of Duchess County, New York, whose enterprises expanded north on the Hudson River close to Glen Falls. Angry over the loss of their mills and mansions to Patriots, the siblings pressed, petitioned and persevered until successive governors of Canada, Carleton and Haldimand, could no longer refuse them their commissions. Once in the soldierly fold, their family defended Canada over several generations—Edward's son and grandson fought in the War of 1812 and Prescott's Battle of the Windmill in 1838, respectively.

Captain Simon Fraser's father died in a rebel prison in Albany after his capture as a British combatant. The family was obliged to head to Canada, where the younger Fraser eventually joined the North West Company, which later merged with its rival, the Hudson's Bay Company. He became a western explorer and followed the river that now bears his name to found Canada's first permanent settlements west of the Rockies. His overland trek to the West Coast of North America followed shortly after those of Canadian Sir Alexander Mackenzie and Americans Meriwether Lewis and William Clarke.

Captain John Deserontyon was overshadowed by Joseph and Molly Brant, though the valor of this Mohawk chief was no less remarkable. Almost single-handedly, he saved the Queen Anne silver, the cherished icon of Christian Mohawk traditions in New York, from falling into Patriot hands. Queen Anne had gifted the silver to the "Four Iroquois Kings" during their visit to England in 1710, and Deserontyon protected and recovered the silver at the risk of his life. The silver communion set is found to this day in the Mohawk chapels near the aptly named towns of Deseronto and Brantford, Ontario.

Lieutenant Henry Simmons was a farmer of Dutch extraction who lived near Hudson and fought at Saratoga. He left his ancestral home to fight in August 1777, but the war ended quickly for him and thousands like him in October at the battles of Freeman's Farm and Bemis Heights, together known as the Battle of Saratoga. Afterward, it took seven weeks for him to lead his twenty-eight men through rough terrain and inclement weather to reach Canada and seven long years for him to secure them lands east of Kingston, where he founded the village of Ernestown. The precise location of his grave site remains unknown, but he is thought to rest ignobly in a backyard of one of his modern-day descendants.

Colonel Joel Stone's story resonates with the sensibilities of modern North Americans: he was a hard-driving entrepreneur for whom family relations sometimes became secondary. He fought rebels as hard as he worked his businesses and endured wounding, imprisonment and a shipwreck near his base on New York's Long Island. Exiled, he went first to Britain and then to Canada to start his life and enterprises anew. Sadly, his wives suffered as he banished his first back to New York and his second was crippled by a musket ball fired by an American soldier during the War of 1812 in a raid on Gananoque, the Canadian town he founded.

Molly Brant was of aristocratic native stock from New York's Mohawk Valley. Few native women before or since have held such influence. One of her male contemporaries by the name of Daniel Klaus said, "One word from her is more taken notice…than a thousand from any white Man without Exception," according to historian and New Yorker James Thomas Flexner. Unfairly remembered by some as merely the consort of Sir William Johnson, she was his life partner, equal to him in all ways but corporal. Her support of the defeated British, who eventually rewarded her with a fine home and pension, led to scorn in some quarters of the Iroquois Confederacy. Like so many others of her time, the precise location of her churchyard grave in Kingston, Ontario, is unknown.

Dr. George Smyth was a physician from Fort Edward, New York, who was secretly a spymaster in the British army's Northern Department under the code name of "Hudibras." He operated literally and figuratively in a rebel hospital in Albany, despite his earlier capture and imprisonment as an enemy intelligence officer. In peacetime, his abridged name lent itself to Smith Falls, a town he was never to see, on the Rideau Canal fifty miles south of Ottawa.

Despite his birth to wealth, education and prestige, Sir John Johnson was no dilettante. He inherited his father's baronetcy, some of the largest landholdings in New York, and the responsibility for tenant farmers. With emboldened rebels closing in on his estate, he fled to safety in Montreal, and despite having arrived exhausted and famished, he took up pursuit of a fleeing party of American attackers. He was commissioned as regiment leader of the King's Loyal Rangers of New York and returned to fight in, and eventually to raze, the Mohawk Valley. Johnson saw to it that thousands of Loyalists were resettled in Canada, and upon his death, his burial crypt on Mount Johnson, now Mont-Saint-Grégoire in Quebec, was deliberately situated to face his beloved New York.

Johnson and the ten other shadow soldiers contained in these pages were not ones of Canadian deity or American demonry as once taught in each country's schools. Nor were they the black-and-white caricatures of North American history for whom America was their loss or Canada their victory. They were merely eleven young men and women who came of age in their New York homeland only to lose it in a war for the ages.

Chapter 1

SERGEANT RICE HONEYWELL

American Continental army sergeant Rice Honeywell of colonial Fredericksburg, New York, might have been a Patriot hero had he not fallen in love with the daughter of a Tory spy. Following his service in the Revolutionary War, Honeywell and his bride-to-be joined her Loyalist parents in Canada, where he eventually made his fortune while his son pioneered the future city of Ottawa, the capital of Canada.

Rice Honeywell's charmed life placed him at the scene of several storied battles in the American Revolution. As a quintessential Yankee entrepreneur, he was inclined toward risk and often let chance define his fate. Honeywell's early life had been that of a Patriot and Continental soldier and officer in New York; his later years were characterized by shrewd land speculation and financial opportunism in Canada. In all cases, Rice Honeywell rarely failed to roll the dice.

In many ways, his luck was intertwined with that of the American general under whom he served longest, Israel Putnam, and that of the first British general he fought on American soil, Sir William Howe. Both leaders were renowned for their daring, in their early careers in particular.

Putnam had been a successful Connecticut farmer and tavern owner who ascended the ranks of the British military quickly and achieved the level of major during the French and Indian War in 1758. He served as commander of Connecticut forces when they attacked Pontiac, the Ottawa chief, and helped bring an end to his siege of Detroit. On one occasion in New York, Putnam was captured by Caughnawaga natives, bound to a tree and saved from being burned alive by the efforts of a French officer. He led regiments attacking Fort Ticonderoga on Lake Champlain and the city of Montreal on the St. Lawrence River and survived a shipwreck in the Caribbean Sea.

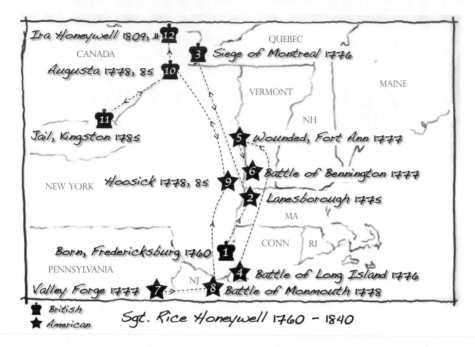

Rice Honeywell was born in Fredericksburg, New York (1), in 1760 and died in 1852 in Augusta Township (10) on the north shore of the St. Lawrence River. *Map by the author.*

About 1766, his stripes as an American Patriot first showed when he helped found the then secretive society of the Sons of Liberty.

Major General Israel Putnam is often attributed with the phrase "Don't fire until you see the whites of their eyes" during the Battle of Bunker Hill. It is little wonder that he inspired Rice Honeywell to name his first son Israel following the Revolutionary War.

In contrast, Putnam's counterpart Sir William Howe had bought his way into English military service as a standard-bearer in 1746 at the age of seventeen. He served as a lieutenant in the War of Austrian Succession and later commanded—and was commended for—a daring landing in the French and Indian War during the siege of Louisburg in Nova Scotia in 1758. The next year, he was instrumental in the British victory at Quebec, which effectively ended France's control of North America. In Europe, he helped capture Belle Isle off the coast of France, and in the Caribbean he was a senior officer during the capture of Havana.

In the mid-1770s in North America, Rice Honeywell threw himself into this mix. By 1775, Howe had succeeded General Thomas Gage as commander in chief of the British army, only six months after Israel

Sergeant Rice Honeywell

Feats at Bunker Hill (pictured) and elsewhere made General Israel Putnam an American folk hero. Members of his extended family were Loyalists who settled in the same region of Canada as Rice Honeywell.

Putnam was said to have walked directly from a field on his farm to join the American rebel forces. Within a year, Putnam would become commander of a force of the American Continental army, and that summer the two men would face each other at the Battle of Bunker Hill. In its aftermath, Howe was shaken with his Pyrrhic victory, but Putnam's moral victory only emboldened him further.

When the two war-hardened officers confronted each other in 1766 at the Battle of Long Island, Rice Honeywell had come of age. He had been, sixteen years earlier, born in Fredericksburg, New York, near the Connecticut border, and according to family biographers, he was of its fifth generation, descended from Roger Hunnewell, who had arrived from England early in the seventeenth century. His antecedents and siblings had met with the sad fates common to New World arrivals—they were lost at sea, killed in battle or felled by the "fever." Others had been more fortunate. His rugged grandfather, who, according to family folklore, was a noted "Indian fighter," lent a hardy reputation to the abridged Honeywell name.

The first opportunity for Rice to bear arms for the American cause came in 1775, when his older brother, Isaiah, who had drilled as a minuteman in Lanesborough, Massachusetts, encouraged fifteen-year-old Rice to join him in Colonel Seth Warner's extra-continental regiment. That winter, the brothers were among the more than four hundred men who trudged to Canada under the command of General Benedict Arnold. By spring, several hundred of Arnold's men had died from a smallpox blight that ravaged the regiment's seven companies. The remaining men were sent to the Isle of Orleans to help cut off incoming British ships, but they were eventually forced to retreat.

Undaunted, Rice returned to Massachusetts and reenlisted under the command of Enoch Poor, who as a young British private had helped expel Acadians from Canada twenty years earlier. It was in General Poor's brigade that Honeywell first benefited from the remarkable bravery of American general Putnam in his showdown on Long Island with British general Sir William Howe on August 27, 1776.

That day, Howe defeated the new commander in chief of the American Continental army, General George Washington, in the Battle of Long Island, an engagement considered the harshest of the Revolutionary War. The British incurred four hundred casualties; the Americans, twenty-seven hundred. What remained of Washington's young but ragtag army was exposed and divided between both sides of New York's East River. Honeywell fought in this conflict, also known as the Battle of Brooklyn Heights, and fled to the island along with Washington and the majority of his troops.

Sergeant Rice Honeywell

British general Sir William Howe underestimated American generals Washington and Putnam following their defeat at Long Island. They led their men to safety in a silent crossing of the East River while Howe's forces slept.

The victorious Howe ignored his British advisors. Rather than stage an immediate and final attack against the vulnerable Americans, he chose to keep his powder dry. As Howe positioned the British army for a siege, Washington devised a plan in which Putnam would lead a stealth evacuation of the American troops across the river from Manhattan to Brooklyn while Howe's forces slept. Under cover of fog, Putnam's men were forbidden to speak in a silent running of the river. Their oars were wrapped in shirts so as not to alert the enemy camped just yards away. At dawn, the Americans were rejoined in Brooklyn, and Howe's British forces crossed the river to find an empty Manhattan encampment. Howe was incredulous that the massively outnumbered Americans had found a way to slip past his troops. His miscalculation may have cost the British their best chance to destroy the rebel army, end the war and retain the colonies.

Within a twenty-four-hour period, seventeen-year-old Rice Honeywell had experienced the rousing yet woeful nature of war. Fortune had favored him and his fellow Continentals during Putnam's risky evacuation, yet only hours earlier, legions of unfortunate Americans had been killed or wounded by Howe's forces.

The Battle of Bennington has two major monuments: the Bennington Battle Monument (pictured), the tallest man-made structure in Vermont, and the Bennington Battlefield State Historic Site, just across the border in Walloomsac, New York, the actual venue of the battle. *Courtesy of Kelly Hunter.*

Sergeant Rice Honeywell

Within a year, Honeywell was back in action and was wounded while skirmishing near Fort Ann, New York, with an advance unit of British general John Burgoyne's southbound army. He was said to have fought "with his arm in a sling," and though his wound hadn't healed, he took up arms soon thereafter with Colonel Seth Warner in the American victory at Bennington, Vermont, in August 1777.

Honeywell gambled that he could turn a dire situation into a profitable one during his final tours of duty in 1778. Throughout the war, it was common practice for men of means to pay middle-class or poor men to substitute for them in order to avoid the draft. Substitute soldiers bet that the double payment—they received their army salaries in addition to money from their benefactors—was worth putting their lives at risk.

Honeywell could not have foreseen what awaited him as a substitute in the winter of 1777–78: several horrific months in destitute, disease-ridden Valley Forge, Pennsylvania. There, ten thousand American troops wintered with grossly inadequate food and clothing. One-third of the Patriot soldiers were so ill that they were later declared unfit for duty; another twenty-five hundred died from typhoid, dysentery and pneumonia. Honeywell survived but in a weakened, vulnerable state.

The United States Memorial Arch at Valley Forge was designed by French-American architect Paul Philippe Cret. The structure is based on the arch of Titus in Rome. *Sketch by the author.*

Renewed by the spring weather and dogged training of Prussian officer Baron de Kalb, the Americans headed east from their bedeviled winter home only to be set upon by the British in June at Monmouth, New Jersey. The battle involved more than thirteen thousand troops on each side, and both considered the victory to be theirs. Soon afterward, Rice Honeywell, still feeling the effects of Valley Forge, fell seriously ill and spent his final military days recovering on furlough.

In 1778, Honeywell lived in the quiet New York hamlet of Hoosick on the edge of the Vermont border where, according to historian Norman Crowder, "he was in love with a young lady, however, whose father was a 'Tory,' and who was obliged to fly to Canada after the close of the war." The lady was Ruth Allen, daughter of Weston Allen, whom Crowder described as a "crippled but energetic Loyalist."

Allen, like Honeywell, was of old New England stock, his family having emigrated from Somerset, England, to Sandwich, Massachusetts, early in the seventeenth century. Allen himself was a self-described "lame man" who, in his Loyalist petition in 1807, claimed that he "did all in his power and…assisted and victualled those of his Magesties troops when on Secret Service." Allen's support of the frontier spies who gathered military intelligence for the British army's Northern Department was well known and made him a target of rebel reprisals. To end his collaborations, Patriots charged him with treason, confiscated his land and forced him to post an enormous bond. Allen continued to aid the British forces, but eventually the intimidation forced him to flee with his family to the safety of Canada and settle on the north shore of the St. Lawrence in Augusta Township, near modern-day Prescott, Ontario.

A descendant of Allen's quoted Rice Honeywell in a written defense of Allen's Loyalist status:

> *After the defeat of General Burgoin he was stript of his property, put under bonds of two thousand pounds with two suffiscant surityes that he should keep within certain bounds and that he should not joine the british forces any more.*

Rice Honeywell and Ruth Allen left Hoosick for Canada to rejoin her family. Honeywell was torn between his marriage and his birth country and they made a brief return to Hoosick in 1785. Many business opportunities awaited Honeywell in the newly formed United States, but his wife pined for her parents, and they returned to Augusta Township in Grenville County on the north shore of the St. Lawrence. Scores of enterprising American

Sergeant Rice Honeywell

Patriots made similar treks to Canada, more often than not drawn by the allure of cheap land. Honeywell acquired his first one hundred acres and began to amass substantial holdings through purchases and land grants. He brought slaves, along with his wife and two children, cleared his land and built a homestead.

His luck turned sour—as it did for all settlers—two years later, during "the hungry year," when a dry spring led to a failed crop and brought starvation conditions to the winter of 1787–88. Many had to slaughter their animals or eat the next year's seeds and grain to survive. Honeywell endured starvation that winter exactly ten years after he had done so at Valley Forge.

Honeywell and his family withstood the famine, and as his holdings added up, so did his problems. American settlers were frequently viewed with suspicion by their Loyalist neighbors. Even Justus Sherwood, the accomplished Green Mountain Boy from Vermont who turned British spymaster and later served as an Upper Canadian justice of the peace, was dressed down by Lord Haldimand for laying out villages with Yankee-style town squares. Sherwood's nemesis was a former New York judge, John Munro, who held a longstanding grudge from the early days of the war and was behind accusations brought against Sherwood's friend Rice Honeywell.

According to historian Mary Beacock Fryer, Honeywell was accused of sedition in 1792 and charged and imprisoned in Kingston after allegedly saying, "Goddamn King George. I have served with Congress." Munro claimed that Honeywell had been "detected in treasonous conversation… a design to burn the King's garrison at Oswegatchie." He also chastised Sherwood for granting "settler status" to the American Honeywell in the first place with an initial grant of one hundred acres.

Apart from returning to the United States every Fourth of July to celebrate the American victory, Honeywell was a settler in good standing. His aggressiveness and opportunism, though considered rough and contrary to Canadian sensibilities, were not treasonous. Honeywell was released on bail and the charges were dropped.

Honeywell's Canadian holdings continued to grow. Ruth received a grant of two hundred acres as the daughter of a Loyalist. Rice bought acreage on the Rideau and Ottawa Rivers and acquired a knack for buying and developing mill sites. He went after locations such as Merrickville on the Rideau River and later leased land at its junction with the Ottawa. By 1807, his holdings exceeded four thousand acres, and according to historian Bruce Elliot, "His prosperity was reflected in a house boasting five fireplaces." Along with other Loyalist settlers, Honeywell sponsored the establishment of the Blue Church on the banks of the St. Lawrence. The grave site of

Rice Honeywell was viewed with suspicion, as were most Americans living in Canada after the Revolutionary War. He spent time in a prison in Kingston, Upper Canada (modern-day southern Ontario), accused of sedition.

Barbara Heck, considered the patron of the Methodist Church in Canada, is found there.

Honeywell's son Ira acquired his father's expansionist ways. In 1809, he made his way north along the Rideau River to the virgin acreage on the south shore of the Ottawa River. He was five miles east of where Colonel John By would select Entrance Bay as the most northerly portal to the Rideau Canal years later. At the time Honeywell pioneered there, there were no other settlers in the nearby area.

The young Honeywell cleared four acres, built a homestead—a far cry from his father's stone mansion—and returned to the St. Lawrence to organize his family for the difficult return journey. In 1811, his wife, son (Rice Jr.) and daughters set out toward the Rideau with all their belongings. The Honeywells built a "jumper" sled consisting of rough-hewn planks on top of tree branches serving as runners. The sled was drawn by oxen from Prescott in Augusta Township, and the family spent their first night at a settlement created by members of General Israel Putnam's extended family near Merrickville, about fifty miles south of the Ottawa River.

They eventually found and pioneered on the south bank of the Ottawa River, where their son John was the first white child to be born in the region.

Sergeant Rice Honeywell

Rice Honeywell was the second owner of the property known as the Clarke Homestead on the Rideau River in Manotick, Ontario, just south of Ottawa. It was the author's home until 2007. *Painting courtesy of Linda Chuimera.*

Sadly, he would also become the first death in Nepean Township in Carleton County two years later.

In 1812, first-term American president James Madison declared war on Britain and began military attacks on Canada. The United States' young economy had been suffering from British impediments and indignities, such as the seizing of American ships, seamen and supplies during the Napoleonic Wars. The British government even continued to maintain outposts in American territory, such as Fort Oswegatchie on the New York side of the St. Lawrence River. Ironically, Madison's war hurt the robust economy of Americans and Canadians who traded back and forth across the river.

Hostilities began with American troops and militiamen engaging British regulars, Canadian militia and native Indian warriors up and down both sides of the river. The action affected the Honeywells on the Ottawa River as a war-induced flour shortage put the family at risk. Ira Honeywell and his son walked sixty miles to the St. Lawrence to obtain food and flour from the family patriarch, Rice. Ira had the supplies hauled by jumper to where the

This interpretation shows a rough-cut log homestead typical of the era when Ira Honeywell settled on the southern shore of the Ottawa River in 1808. The tiny settlement he founded eventually grew to become Ottawa, Canada's capital city. *Sketch by the author.*

road ended at Merrickville, floated them by raft the rest of the distance to the Hogs Back rapids on the Rideau and "bushed" out a road to finally get them to his wife and daughters, who were near starvation.

The family toughed out the next few years living in their one-story cabin. The logs were chinked in moss and clay, the floor and fireplace were made of stone and their oxen were housed in an attached lean-to. The Honeywells used their steers to get through the winter snow and later bought the first horse and wagon in the settlement that was to become Bytown and later, Ottawa. Ira's bush road had become passable, owing to the loggers who used it to get in and out of the woods. Thanks to his munificent father, they had glass-paned windows (most settlers could only afford oiled paper) and the luxury of a four-poster canopy bed, which they hauled all the way to the Ottawa River from the St. Lawrence.

They eventually moved back from the river, as his wife, Polly Honeywell, was increasingly unnerved by Indian travelers who simply—according to native custom—walked into their home when passing by. In 1819, Ira built his second home, and his entrepreneurial instincts led him to establish a ferry to the north side of the river.

Sergeant Rice Honeywell

Within a few years, Colonel John By arrived from England with instructions from the Duke of Wellington to build a canal from the Ottawa River to Kingston to serve as an alternative route back and forth to Montreal in the event that any future American attack cut off the St. Lawrence. Since there were only a few settlements scattered along the largely unpopulated Rideau corridor, Colonel By and his men were able to build their canal system using spillways to flood lowlands and flow water over waste weirs alongside the canal locks.

Such a canal system would not have been practical in the more densely populated United States, where provisioning towns along the Erie Canal had already put New York City on the path to becoming the country's biggest port. The scattered settlements in Canada meant that the English engineers, Scottish masons and Irish laborers had to overcome onerous topography in locations often difficult to supply. Colonel By also had to deal with canny and obstreperous land speculators, including Rice Honeywell, who acquired Rideau frontage from Loyalists who considered their grants to be worthless wilderness. Honeywell often bought land for a pittance and used his titles to leverage hefty returns.

When the canal was finished in 1832, the threat of another invasion from south of the border had all but passed. Rice Honeywell, American soldier, expatriate and Canadian entrepreneur, died with his fortune intact in 1839 and is assumed to be buried in an unmarked grave by the Blue Church in Augusta Township.

Rice Honeywell's son, Ira, was the first settler in the future capital of Canada. Ironically, he returned to live in the United States, where he died in 1852.

Chapter 2

CAPTAIN JOSEPH BRANT

Joseph Brant had the mind of a statesman and the soul of a warrior, and had the British prevailed, New York might have remained his homeland. Instead, he wreaked ferocity on it from within America and brought vengeance to it from Canada.

Joseph Brant's Mohawk name of *Thayendanegen* translated to "he who binds two sticks together" and corresponded with his dream for the Iroquois Confederacy to live in peace and equality with whites. It implied that his calling card to British, French and American whites was diplomacy, just as it was with the other Indian nations of the confederacy—the Senecas, Oneidas, Onondagas, Cayugas and (later) Tuscaroras.

But Brant's name had a more ominous duality: he negotiated with those he could and waged brutal war against those he couldn't. The only exception among the whites were the British, for they had raised and educated him.

In the Seven Years' War in the 1750s and '60s, known as the French and Indian War in North America, Brant stood with the British to help defeat the French. He stood alongside them again during the Revolutionary War in the 1770s and '80s but was defeated by Patriots in the American rebel colonies. In the end, he was considered a ruthless combatant by the Americans, an enemy to the French, a pawn to be undercut by the British during peace negotiations in Paris and, to the Canadians, a hero who settled his people peaceably between Lakes Erie and Ontario in Upper Canada in what is now the province of Ontario. History records, however, no instance of him performing or encouraging atrocities.

Brant was born in 1741 by the Ohio River. His mother Margaret's ancestral home was the Mohawk Valley, but her husband, Peter, brought her and her daughter Molly, among others, west in search of fur. Upon his death,

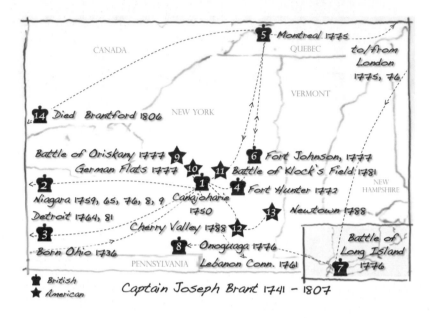

Joseph Brant was a teenager when he moved from the Ohio Valley to Canajoharie (1) along the Mohawk River. After the war, he established a Canadian community for displaced Mohawks on the Grande River near the western tip of Lake Ontario (14). *Map by the author.*

Margaret returned with her children to Canajoharie, New York, and married a man by the name of Brant, whose surname Molly and Joseph adopted.

Joseph Brant was in his mid-teens when he saw his first action about 120 miles northeast of Canajoharie at the Battle of Lake George, a long thin lake at the base of the Adirondack Mountains in northern New York. He later confided with his sister that his first war experience was so harrowing that he clung to a tree to steady himself. He managed to corral his nerves and eventually engaged the enemy.

It is likely that Joseph was known by that time to Sir William Johnson, the leader of the English and Indian contingent at the Battle of Lake George. Johnson, who had romantically associated himself with Molly, was Brant's future mentor and became a baronet as a result of the British victory. By the time he assumed the role of superintendant of Indian affairs in 1756, Johnson was one of the wealthiest landowners and most influential men in the New York colony.

The French and Indian War had been an opportunity for the genial and astute Johnson to emerge as a great friend of the natives. Compared to a series of blundering British military commanders, Johnson emerged

Captain Joseph Brant

George Romney, a mid-eighteenth-century English portraitist, painted Joseph Brant in London in 1776. Brant had gone to England on behalf of the Iroquois Confederacy to negotiate redress for lost lands in the Mohawk and Susquehanna Valleys.

as a fresh and forthright face, a renaissance man who foresaw the need to cultivate and educate native leaders of the future.

Joseph Brant matured into a native warrior over a succession of battles: with Johnson again at the Battle of Fort Niagara in 1757 and with Sir Jeffery Amherst as he placed a siege on Montreal in 1760. After this engagement, Brant was one of many natives rewarded by the British with a silver medal.

Following Niagara and Montreal, Brant earned Johnson's attention for his agility in both mind and body. In 1861, Brant was sent with two other Mohawk teens on a six-hundred-mile trip to attend Moor's Charity School for Indians in Lebanon, Connecticut, so named for one of its benefactors. Brant studied under Reverend Ebenezer Wheelock, who later founded Dartmouth College and with whom Brant remained friends for the rest of the preacher's days, despite differing strongly on the politics of revolution. Brant was educated in the classics of history and literature and became an Anglican missionary, while the other two Mohawks boys, for various reasons, disengaged.

Charity schools in England in the eighteenth century were a means of caring for and educating dispossessed children. Though less common in North America, some prospered, like Ebenezer Wheelock's Moors Charity School, where Joseph Brant studied and which grew into Dartmouth College. *Sketch by the author.*

Captain Joseph Brant

Meanwhile, Johnson had emerged as the preeminent manager of relations with the Indian nations and had to deal with the backfiring of King George's Royal Proclamation of 1763. The decree was intended to improve relations with the Indians who lived in the former French territory west of the Adirondacks, which, along with Quebec, Florida and Grenada, had been ceded to the English after the Seven Years' War. Accustomed to receiving gifts in their dealings with the French, the natives were being overrun by white settlers and found the British, with the exception of Johnson, to be brittle, overbearing and tightfisted.

Johnson empathized with them and even applauded the French *coureurs de bois* for their honorable dealings among the Iroquois. Less impressive to him was the French scheme to drive the British and Iroquois apart and direct the fur trade through their lands down the Mississippi Valley.

The British proclamation had in part been a response to a fierce uprising led by an Ottawa chief, Pontiac, in which forts and villages were burned and settlers were killed and scalped. Brant had planned to go to New York City to continue his studies at the highly regarded King's College but instead was called home by Johnson. Rather than being surrounded by white students and lecturers, Brant was encircled by two thousand natives and sachems in a successful grand parlay led by Johnson at Fort Niagara to end the war.

By that time, Brant's sister Molly had become Johnson's intimate, living in and managing his estate, Johnson Hall. Molly may have been fearful for Joseph's life, and she may have played a part in bringing Brant home to New York from Connecticut. Despite the increasing Anglicization of the Brants and their partial adoption of the English language, education and customs, they remained Mohawk first and foremost. Joseph Brant never returned to Wheelock's school.

Brant's dualistic nature couldn't help but emerge at this time. Johnson oversaw the Indian council at Niagara, resplendent in full Iroquois regalia, and Brant was very impressed at the positive effects of this gesture. In 1764, Brant went on the attack again at Fort Detroit and saw the role violence played in eventually leading Pontiac to a truce. These events helped shape Brant into a man who bound together the "two sticks" of diplomacy and war.

A nineteenth-century passage from the journal of an American combatant in the Revolutionary War offered a chilling yet impressive description of Brant. The American had witnessed Brant, who had adopted Johnson's habit of mixing British and Mohawk garb, in the presence of prisoners:

> *He was a likely fellow, of a fierce aspect—tall and rather spare—well spoken, and apparently about thirty [forty] years of age. He wore*

moccasins, elegantly trimmed with beads—leggings and breech-cloth of superfine blue—short green-coat, with two silver epaulets—and a small, laced, round hat. By his side hung an elegant silver-mounted cutlass...he replied—"That is my fighting ground...You are young, and you I pity; but for that old villain there," pointing at the father, "I have no pity."

Brant's increasing maturity led him back to Canajoharie, where he married the daughter of an Oneida leader, started a family and moved into his deceased stepfather's large home on the south bank of the Mohawk River. By the end of the decade, however, Brant had become a widower. He married again—this time to his deceased wife's sister—but she, too, soon died. His third wife was the daughter of a colorful fur trader, George Crogan, who was born in Ireland and, like Johnson, had immigrated to America. Crogan had come to New York the year Brant was born and became a successful fur trader in the Ohio Valley before the French moved in. He survived a hatchet to the head during Pontiac's Rebellion and eventually became Johnson's deputy superintendent of Indian affairs.

Brant's career advanced during his early years of marriage. Under Johnson's wing, he became a superb interpreter of the many languages within the Iroquois Confederacy found between Lake Champlain and Niagara. In 1771, he moved east along the Mohawk to its junction with the Schoharie River at Fort Hunter. He began a long association with Reverend John Stewart, who encouraged him to seclude himself in the fort's parsonage to translate Anglican scripture into the Mohawk language.

Once the scripture had been translated, Brant returned to Canajoharie and was encouraged by Johnson to more fully embrace his tribal hierarchy, which he did. He was made a war chief and primary spokesman of the Mohawk, but in 1774 his great friend and mentor General Sir William Johnson died of a stroke at his nearby estate, Johnson Hall.

The deceased baronet's son John inherited the title and estate, but it was his nephew and son-in-law Guy Johnson who succeeded William as superintendent of northern Indian affairs. Guy Johnson was both temperamentally and physically Joseph's lesser: he was obstinate, short, pudgy and topped with a powdered wig. Brant was garrulous, tall, patrician in bearing and kept his head partially shaved and feathered. Johnson, however, was astute enough to know that Brant excelled at native interpretation and commissioned him as a captain in the military and as his private secretary. Tellingly, Brant was always to enter battle as a Mohawk war chief rather than as a captain in the British army.

Captain Joseph Brant

The building in which Joseph Brant translated parts of the New Testament into the Mohawk tongue still stands. The stone structure was built in 1734 just to the east of Fort Hunter in the Mohawk Valley. *Sketch by the author.*

As Patriot forces began moving into the Mohawk Valley in the spring of 1775, Guy Johnson and more than 120 Loyalists, along with Brant and most of the Indian warriors from Canajoharie, escaped to British-held Montreal. By autumn, Guy Johnson, riled at the undermining of his authority from London, had taken Brant, as well as Loyalists Gilbert Tice and Captain John Deserontyon (the game Mohawk officer from Fort Hunter), to England. Johnson lobbied for control of Indian affairs in the northern colonies but was only partially successful. The real headliner turned out to be Brant, who met with King George III, strode around London in his Mohawk outfits, became a Mason, sat for a soon-to-be-famous portrait by renowned artist George Romney and generally became a British *cause célèbre*.

The influential English voices heard by Brant spoke of war. The violence that had begun when British troops fired on unarmed Patriots in the Boston Massacre of 1770 finally sparked in Lexington and Concord in 1775 and escalated into full-scale rebellion. Brant saw the opportunity to gain leverage

Joseph Brant's diplomacy gave way to his pugilistic instincts shortly after his return from England in the summer of 1776. He was a combatant in the Battle of Long Island that August. Print, 1800s.

and extracted promises for Mohawk land in return for support of the British during the conflict.

Satisfied with his deal, Brant returned to North America at Staten Island and entered the war during the Battle of Long Island. Afterward, and in disguise, he headed north and west with Tice to Onoquaga, near Binghamton, New York, where he had placed his family for safety while he was out of the colony. The reunion was short-lived, as Brant headed farther west toward Niagara to round up British support from the Iroquois Confederacy. Also known as the Six Nations (the Tuscarora had joined the original five earlier in the 1700s), the native confederacy that had lasted hundreds of years began to crack under the weight of the revolution.

Patriot forces hadn't reached out to the natives for support. General George Washington initially prohibited them from joining the American Continental army. As it was, most natives believed the rebellion to be a "white man's" war and preferred to remain neutral. Brant's argument was that native ancestral lands would be in jeopardy if the Americans were victorious. The Oneidas and Tuscaroras, thinking that Brant and the Mohawks were overvalued, sided with the Patriots. In response, Brant set up supply depots at Onoquaga and Unadilla on the Susquehanna River and commissioned scouting parties to gather intelligence and raiding parties to collect food. In addition to the Mohawks, he had been successful in lining up the Senecas and Onondagas behind the British. War chiefs Sayenqueraghta, or "Old Smoke," and Cornplanter led the Senecas and were originally considered senior to Brant.

The stage was set for natives to fight natives. In August 1777, at Oriskany in the Mohawk Valley, Brant and Sir John Johnson, now head of his own King's Royal Regiment of New York, were sent on a mission to intercept the Tyron County militia moving west with Oneida warriors to break a British siege of Fort Stanwix. The Mohawks and Senecas disregarded Johnson's orders to stand their ground and instead moved with Loyalists to trap General Nicholas Herkimer and his Oneida allies in a smaller valley. After several hours of fighting, tamed only by an hour-long thunderstorm, Herkimer was badly wounded, and his casualties, including the natives, outnumbered those of his enemy by three to one.

It was a Pyrrhic victory for Brant and the Loyalists. The British siege of Stanwix didn't hold, and by October the forces of General John Burgoyne—for whom the siege formed part of his assault from the west—had been defeated by the Americans at Saratoga and surrendered. Undaunted, Brant raised a force of several hundred Indians and Loyalists and undertook a series of violent raids that earned him the damning name among the Patriots of "Monster Brant." Brant was equally disparaging of the Patriot Committees of Safety of local militia. Loyalist farms were being confiscated and the owners thrown into vermin-infested prisons. Rebel jails in Albany, New York, and Litchfield, Connecticut, and the copper mines of Simsbury near the Massachusetts border were particularly notorious.

In September 1788, Brant's Volunteers, along with Loyalist rangers, attacked German Flats in the Mohawk Valley. Homes were destroyed, farms were despoiled, mills were burned and only a warning by a survivor of a doomed scouting party dispersed the residents before any physical cruelty could be dealt out.

This was not the case two months later, in November 1788, when Brant grudgingly joined the son of Lieutenant Colonel John Butler in an attack of retribution on the undefended village of Cherry Valley. Whether the circumstances that permitted the Seneca warriors to attack first were deliberate or not was unclear, but the result left the undefended town in ruins and many of its men, woman and children tomahawked and scalped. For many years afterward, Brant was thought responsible for the atrocities. Although he did participate in the raid—motivated in part by the Patriot razing of his own village and supply depots—he was vindicated of overseeing the harshness and the butchery.

Continental soldiers carried out a "scorched earth" campaign against Mohawk villages as retribution for the destruction of American communities earlier in the war. Print, 1800s.

Brant continued his raids and prevailed whenever he encountered opposition, and he always called for the sparing of women and children. In the summer of 1779, he entered the Neversink Valley at the base of the Catskills and destroyed farms and houses. A poorly equipped and comparatively untrained Patriot militia tried to ambush Brant and his seasoned volunteers a few days later but was outmatched, defeated and suffered heavy casualties. Brant's successes were not unnoticed by the man with whom he had dealt in London, Lord Germaine. Germaine promoted him to colonel, though his commission was not passed along by the governor of Canada, Sir Fredrick Haldimand, perhaps out of politics or deference to the Seneca chiefs.

Brant's day of reckoning came the following year in a move of sound strategic judgment for which George Washington was becoming known. Washington ordered General John Sullivan and a force of several thousand Continental soldiers to engage the Iroquois raiding parties, raze their villages, destroy their crops and deny them future subsistence. They did so effectively in the Allegheny, Susquehanna and Mohawk Valleys while fending off guerilla attacks by the Iroquois. Brant, perhaps rightly, felt that raids on the larger American force would be more effective in slowing Sullivan down than a direct assault. All told, more than forty Onondaga,

Captain Joseph Brant

This memorial in Brantford, Ontario, reads "THAYENDANEGEA: Capt. Joseph Brant, born 1742, died 1807, interred at the Mohawk Church and to the Six Nations Indians for their long and faithful services on behalf of the British Crown and their strict observance to treaties." Print, 1800s.

Seneca and Mohawk villages were destroyed in the American general's wake. The Iroquois faced Sullivan down but were utterly defeated in the Battle of Newtown, near modern-day Elmira, New York, in August 1779. Many of the survivors straggled to Fort Niagara and faced a devastating winter without food or shelter.

The next year, Brant wreaked his vengeance, and with a refreshed force, he descended from Canada and wiped out every white settlement from Schenectady to Ohio. He was similarly merciless with the Patriot-aligned Oneida and Tuscarora villages.

He counterpunched again but was wounded in a raid known as the Battle of Klock's Field, and in 1781 he successfully defended Fort Detroit against U.S. general George Roger Clark. In October of that year, his dreams of an Iroquois dominion came to an end with word that the British had been defeated by the Americans, aided by the French, at Yorktown.

Brant was a relatively young and able man at the end of the war (his only wound had been to his heel). During peace negotiations, he and John Deserontyon felt that the British were guilty of betrayal with the Treaty of Paris in 1783, though in truth, the Mohawk lands had been ceded twenty years earlier in George III's proclamation, to which the Iroquois had agreed. A remorseful Haldimand compensated both men in 1784 with money and land grants in Canada—Deserontyon accepted property on the northern shore of Lake Ontario and Brant took land at its western tip, closer to the Seneca homeland.

Much of his efforts over the next three decades were aimed at protecting the Six Nations' land from Canadian and British finagling. Ironically, the "Monster Brant" became a confidant of the "Town Destroyer" (the Iroquois name for George Washington) in joint efforts to settle native disputes in the United States. Brant also tried in vain to bring a union of self-protection to the American Northwest Indians.

At his very end, Joseph Brant's last words implied that his "two sticks" had finally become unbound. On his deathbed in 1807 in Brantford, in what is modern-day Ontario, he implored his adopted white son to use diplomacy to do good on behalf of "the poor Indians."

Chapter 3

MARY HOOPLE

A pair of pioneer siblings was separated after their abduction by Delaware and Seneca warriors in 1780. More than seventy years passed before they were reunited. During the intervening years, the brother saw action in the War of 1812 and the sister became legendary for her compassion.

In 1851—his 101st year—Jacob Sheets tearfully traded war stories with the nephew he hadn't seen in more than seventy years. His recent blindness kept him from seeing John Whitmore's bittersweet expression during their emotional exchange, which took place near Hoople Creek by the north shore of the St. Lawrence River.

Sheets told Whitmore of the North American Wars of Empire, during which he had served in the King's Royal Regiment of New York in the Grenadier Company led by Sir John Johnson. Whitmore in turn spoke of his days as a captain at the siege of Fort Niagara in the War of 1812 and in the Upper Canada Rebellion of 1837.

Also present at the poignant reunion was John Whitmore's older sister, Mary Hoople, with whom he had been abducted seven decades earlier. In 1780, a murderous raiding party had attacked the family's homestead near the Susquehanna River on the Pennsylvania frontier. Their uncle Jacob had visited them in the year before the Whitmore massacre, and the three had not been together since.

During her uncle's 1779 visit, Mary had met the man who would later become her husband, Henry Hoople. The young man had traveled with Jacob Sheets from the New York colony to the doomed Whitmore family's Pennsylvania homestead in an encounter said to have transfixed them both. Mary and John's maternal relatives were of German origin and had

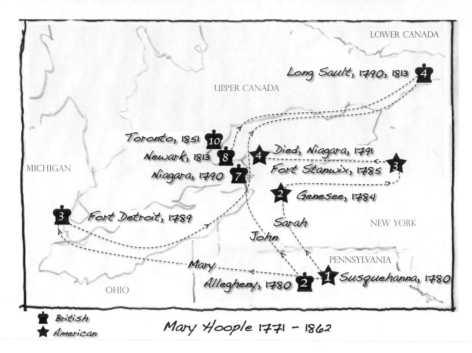

Much of Mary Hoople's long life, which began in the upper Susquehanna Valley (1) and ended near Long Sault (4), was spent with the whereabouts of her brother John Hoople unknown. A chance encounter by her son, a New York City businessman, led to the healing of the emotional wound in 1851. *Map by the author.*

immigrated to Virginia and later Pennsylvania via New Jersey. According to Elizabeth Hoople, Mary's descendant and biographer, the family had experienced an Indian attack generations earlier in the Shenandoah Valley. Mary's great-grandmother had wielded a tomahawk to protect her children from a raiding party after her valorous husband had been killed.

Mary and John's father, Peter Whitmore, was descended from Cromwellian soldiers who had fled England for the Netherlands and then immigrated to America once Charles II accepted the English Crown. A stalwart and hardy pioneer, Peter could not have been prepared for the tragedy that befell his family on Easter Sunday 1780, when a party of Seneca, Delaware and Oneida warriors descended on their cabin, aided by one métis trader.

Peter was shot dead in his bed; his wife was killed and her scalp was removed by hatchet. Philip, the eldest son, was tomahawked as he looked up from the fireplace he had been stoking. Of the remaining children who scattered into the woods, four were caught. Mary and John were taken, and the eldest girl, Sarah, was captured with the youngest sibling, an infant, held protectively in her arms. Their brother Jake never emerged from the forest.

Mary Hoople

Among the perils faced by American colonials was abduction by native peoples. Although motivations varied, the most common were slave labor, extortion and the symbolic absorption of white cultural identity. Print, 1800s.

The children were placed under guard as their homestead was looted and burned. The natives killed the baby by swinging her against a tree. The remaining three Whitmore children were placed on horseback and taken away by their captors.

Two days later, the children were divided between the Senecas and Delawares, Sarah with the former, and Mary and John with the latter. Mary later recalled that she had considered an escape attempt with her younger brother but wisely recognized the gruff and grimacing native warriors to be a safer alternative to the bears and cougars of the forest. By the third day, the two children and their captors had reached a Delaware camp on the Allegheny River. They never saw Sarah again.

Upon their arrival at the camp, eleven-year-old Mary and seven-year-old John were adorned in wampum beadwork, placed at the front of a procession and displayed as prizes by their abductors. They were separated and placed in different lodges until that evening, when they were forced to witness a frightening sight: a war party in which braves danced in full paint and ceremonial clothing and stomped in circles around the campfire, shooting their firearms and waving their hatchets. Their war paint was predominantly black, the symbol of grief, evil and death, and was contrasted with red, symbolizing blood.

The older warriors wore their coarse black hair long to their shoulders; younger men would have plucked their own scalps to fine scalp locks, topped with eagle feathers and held upright by animal grease. The two white children thought it odd that the native men had no beards—their facial hair had been plucked out at the roots with mussel shells serving as tweezers. Smooth faces were easier to paint, with black shale and wood ashes used for the darker shades and red or yellow clay for the lighter.

Mary and John's assimilation had begun. Most of the village inhabitants lived in round birch-bark wigwams with domed roofs topped with gaping holes that served as chimneys for indoor open-pit fires. All slept in sapling beds and sat on benches made of skin-covered branches. The odoriferous, stale smell of bear grease was inescapable, as the huts and wigwams had no windows or air circulation, only a single doorway covered with animal skin. Eventually, after receiving relentless insect bites, the white children realized that the Delaware wore bear grease as bug repellent. The children's homespun pioneer clothes were replaced with bearskin garments in the winter and doeskin in the summer. Like the rest of the villagers, they were shod in deerskin moccasins decorated with colored beads or porcupine quills.

Over time, Mary saw less of John, as his days were spent with the men in preparation for his graduation to the hunters' ranks. Mary had begun bonding with her Delaware mother and joined her in making jewelry from stone, shells, animal teeth and claws. More important, her adoptive mother was a medicine woman who taught the young girl how to make healing balms and salves. Mary's initiation into the practice was to tend to her brother John, who, along with the other Delaware boys, was inducted into the tribe in a ceremony during which his forearms were burned over an open fire. Mary quickly put her hatred for her captors aside and began caring for her tribe as if they were her family. In order to make her bowls of soothing lotions, she foraged—sometimes for weeks—looking for roots and herbs, and the curious red flowers used to cure typhoid, "the white man's fever."

After a medicine-gathering trip in 1784, Mary returned to discover her brother gone; he had been rescued by a British officer. The boy could no longer speak English (or German) and could not convey to the officer that his sister lived in the camp too. Also present at the rescue was the same métis who had participated in the Whitmore massacre: De Coignee. The disreputable tracker and Delaware spy had sold his knowledge of the boy's whereabouts to the British while withholding his information regarding Mary. His lustful

Mary Hoople

Iroquois society was matrilineal and as such differed greatly from white society. In life, an Iroquois mother was the head of the family; in death, family declension began at her graveside. Print, 1800s.

and unseemly presence in the first half of Mary's life was bothersome to her. The Whitmore women were known for their attractiveness, and De Coignee pursued Mary relentlessly, even cajoling the natives in an attempt to force her to marry him at the age of sixteen.

Despite the signing of the Treaty of Paris the previous year, the American Revolutionary War had not entirely ended, and hostilities continued along the Niagara frontier and northwest on the Great Lakes at Forts Detroit and Michilimackinac.

The British held on to several possessions on the grounds that the United States had reneged on aspects of the negotiated settlement. The occupants of the forts were usually British military and English, French and German settlers who suffered no shortages of food and comforts when compared to the native tribes. Every spring, the Delaware found their hunting grounds diminished, thanks to white migration, and were forced to move farther west in search of food.

Mary's adoptive family agreed to travel to Fort Detroit to help the despondent teenager locate her brother and, more importantly, to avoid starvation. Faced with no alternative, the family agreed to sell Mary in return for food. At the age of eighteen, Mary was purchased by a family of French

As young Mary Hoople made her way between Lakes Erie and Ontario, she unknowingly passed by two nephews she was never to meet. The two were American soldiers stationed at Fort Niagara and sons of her then deceased sister, Sarah. Print, 1800s.

settlers for "twelve moons" of servitude within the protective walls of Fort Detroit. For almost a year, Mary served the family of René Chauvin with dedication and often helped nurse war-wounded and sick soldiers, as well as settlers, back to good health.

The fort's twelve-foot stockade seemed confining to Mary as she pined not only for her brother but also for the spacious forests and hunting grounds where she had come of age. She befriended Captain Thomas McKee, son of Colonel McKee, the unsympathetic, austere but gentlemanly commander of Fort Detroit, who rebuffed Mary's requests for assistance in tracking down her missing brother. McKee knew that thousands of whites had been embedded among the frontier tribes and that a search for one freed boy among the many villages and forts would be futile. The colonel's attitude quickly changed after Mary reported the presence of De Coignee in the fort. She revealed to McKee that the métis had been involved in the murder of her parents and that he was known to be a native spy. McKee ordered him arrested, but De Coignee managed to escape.

As the end of Mary's year of servitude approached, a Lutheran pastor arrived at Fort Detroit and made inquiries about a white child named "Mary Whitmoyer." Jacob Sheets had sent the pastor to search among the forts of Lakes Erie and Ontario for his nieces and nephew. Sheets resided along the north shore of the St. Lawrence on land grants that he had received for his service to the "Royal Greens," the King's Royal Regiment of New York.

In return for Mary's loyalty and for nursing his wife through a serious illness, Chauvin relieved her of her last month's servitude. With winter

Mary Hoople

The Long Sault rapids were a significant barrier to navigation of the St. Lawrence River until canal building began in the early nineteenth century. Hoople Creek crosses Ontario's Long Sault Parkway almost directly north of Massena, New York. Print, 1800s.

approaching and ice closing up the lake harbors, Mary hurried the pastor to prepare for the five-hundred-mile journey eastward. The pastor had secured a large canoe with a crew of voyageurs who were headed east to Montreal. With Mary onboard, they paddled down the Detroit River to Lake Erie, portaged around Niagara Falls to Lake Ontario and headed east down the St. Lawrence. Unbeknownst to Mary, when they bypassed Fort Niagara en route to Long Sault, they also passed by her younger brother, who resided inside the fort as the adoptive son of a Canadian officer, Captain Daniel Servos of Butler's Rangers.

Within weeks, Mary was reunited with Jacob Sheets and began to relearn the German language her mother had taught her as a child. In the years ahead, she served as the doctor in Long Sault and used her aboriginal medicines to revive pioneer families who suffered through summers of drought and winters of starvation. Meanwhile, John remained in the Niagara region, married the captain's daughter and created a homestead on the shores of Lake Ontario a few miles west of Newark (Niagara-on-the-Lake).

Mary often cried at the thought of her sister Sarah, who had been taken away by the Senecas after their abduction. Like Mary, Sarah was considered attractive and was sought after as a bride. She was raised Mohawk and spent much of her time in the Genesee Valley of the New York colony, and she sought to avoid the affections of a determined chief. Had they married, she would never have returned to the white settler community.

Sarah met the well-regarded Horatio Jones, who had been a white captive of the Seneca nation. As one of the tribe's English interpreters, he had proved so valuable that he was voted a tribal chief. Sarah sought him out, fell in love and married him. Jones was the son of a New York blacksmith and was considered a formidable frontiersman. He had been included, along with Mary, in the prisoner exchange following the 1784 Treaty of Fort Stanwix. Sarah and Horatio were married in a Christian ceremony on the eve of 1785. Their eldest son was said to be the first white child born in the western half of the New York colony. Sarah gave birth to three more sons, and Jones became the United States government's interpreter with the Seneca nation. Sarah died in 1791, and Jones raised his four boys in the large estate he built on the American side of Niagara.

During the War of 1812, the widower Jones's two youngest sons joined the New York militia and were among the American troops who occupied Newark in 1813. They traveled by boat one evening to visit the man they understood to be their uncle, John Whitmore. They were unaware that the British had moved into a position between Whitmore's homestead and Newark. Whitmore saw his nephews come ashore and, once he realized who they were, became horrified that the boys might be caught behind enemy lines and shot as spies. With the help of a fellow officer, Whitmore spirited the young men back behind their own lines by boat. The two died a week later when the British attacked Fort Niagara with the help of Indian allies who killed and scalped both boys.

In yet another caprice of fate that befell the Whitmores, John was made aware that the métis De Coignee was to travel near his Lake Ontario farm. Armed with his musket and tomahawk, he lay in wait for the Indian spy, with every intention of avenging his family's murder. The opportunity arose as the métis walked the Lake Road past his hiding place, but John demurred and chose to adhere to his Christian beliefs, letting De Coignee live rather than take a shot.

The War of 1812 also came to Mary's doorstep in Long Sault. She had married Henry Hoople, the young man she had met decades earlier when he visited the Whitmore homestead with her uncle Jacob the year before the massacre. The couple lived beside Hoople Creek near the St. Lawrence River and later built a homestead set back from the water and farther into the woods. They raised a large family of boys, many of whom

Mary Hoople

The fourth president of the United States, President James Madison, wrote a letter to Mary Hoople with a significant honorarium and a message of thanks for the compassion she showed a wounded U.S. soldier during the War of 1812. *Sketch by the author.*

would join their father in the Loyalist militia. On November 19, 1813, U.S. general James Wilkinson's soldiers came down the river in the direction of Hoople Creek.

Wilkinson had crossed to the north bank of the St. Lawrence, determined to head downriver to take Montreal. He sent his cavalry troops ahead to Cornwall to seize supplies just as the local militia was mustered. The Loyalists set up an ambush across the creek from the house of Henry Hoople's brother. Mary had been secreted there and was unable to leave before the Americans set up cannons in the front yard. A blazing gun battle ensued, but the Americans were overwhelmed and began their retreat.

Left behind was a wounded young American soldier who was no older than Mary's sons. She emerged from the house and began to attend to his wounds on the property that had been a battlefield only moments earlier. The next day, Wilkinson's troops went down in defeat in the Battle of Chrysler's Farm.

Over the coming months, Mary restored the soldier to good health, and he returned home after the war. When word of her bravery and her compassion for the American soldier was received in Washington, Mary was

On business in Toronto from New York City, Mary Hoople's son William overheard a reference to a man whose history paralleled his mother's. The chance encounter led to a reunion between Mary and her brother after a seventy-year separation. Print, 1800s.

awarded a large sum of money and received a special commendation from U.S. president James Madison.

Almost four decades later, one of her sons, who had become a prosperous merchant in New York City, overheard a story while in Toronto on business: an elderly man by the name of John Whitmore had been abducted by the Delawares as a child and was now living on the southern shore of Lake Ontario. Mary's son located John and organized a steamboat trip in 1851 that took him from Niagara to Long Sault to meet with his lost uncle Jacob and sister Mary.

Two years after their poignant reunion, John Whitmore died at the age of seventy-seven. Mary died in 1862 at the age of ninety-one. The fate of their brother Jake, who ran into the woods the day of the Whitmore massacre, is unknown to this day.

Chapter 4

MAJOR EDWARD JESSUP

Major Edward Jessup was a successful Hudson River entrepreneur whose only losses came during the American Revolution and in the Patriot courts of New York. Eventually, he repeated his success and founded the riverfront village of Prescott on the north shore of the Saint Lawrence River.

L ife in North America unfolded like a three-act play in the second half of the eighteenth century. The theatrics began in 1775 in Lexington, Massachusetts, with the first shots fired between the Patriot militia and the British army. The hostilities escalated into the battle royal that opened the Revolutionary War and climaxed in 1777 at the Battle of Saratoga, New York. The drama's resolution came three years later with the American victory over the British at Yorktown. The final curtain—the denouement—was drawn closed with the Treaty of Paris in 1783.

The life of Edward Jessup followed a similar dramatic arc. His career began as an entrepreneur in the Hudson Valley and grew rapidly until Revolutionary hostilities destroyed his business. He was present to witness the spectacle of General John Burgoyne's British forces surrender at Saratoga. With his future in New York nonexistent, Jessup resolved to live in Canada in exile and did so successfully until 1816, when he succumbed to palsy in Prescott, the town he founded on the north bank of the St. Lawrence River.

Jessup's life had begun more than eighty-one years earlier in Fairfield, Connecticut, a county that had come by its name honestly—it hugged the rocky north shore beach of Long Island Sound, with vast inland forests and workable fields that lay speckled with the traditional dogwood blossoms of yellow and white. Order also bloomed in Fairfield as Connecticut's self-government began there as early as 1639.

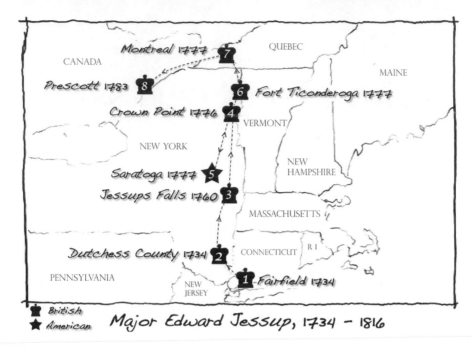

Major Edward Jessup and his brothers embodied the rough and ready entrepreneurial drive that characterized eighteenth-century American businessmen. They brought it to Prescott (8), the community they founded on the Canadian side of the St. Lawrence River. *Map by the author.*

Colonel Edward Jessup's great-grandfather came from England, it is thought, before 1649 and settled in Westchester, New York. According to probate records of Stamford, the patriarch's wife, Elizabeth Hyde, gave birth to Colonel Jessup's grandfather, another Edward, in 1663 in West Haven (then known as West Farms). The town had been founded twenty years earlier by six farmers who had relocated north and east of New York. Like the village of Stamford down shore twenty miles where the Jessups were to later move, West Farms had a stretch of shoreline from which, on a good day, the shadows of Long Island could be seen across the sound. This view had been long enjoyed by the Paugussett natives who harvested the waterfront for oysters. Like most of Connecticut's native peoples, they were almost wiped out by the smallpox that came with the white settlement a few years before the second generation's Edward Jessup was born.

While a young man, Edward Jessup moved southwest along the Long Island Sound and settled in Stamford, where he and his wife, Abigail, began a family. His son Joseph, their firstborn, arrived in 1699. Joseph was to enjoy longevity, as was the family tradition. Joseph's son, also named Edward,

Major Edward Jessup

REVOLUTIONARY MONUMENT AT LEXINGTON, MASS.

REVOLUTIONARY MONUMENT AT CONCORD, MASS.

When word spread that hostilities had broken out in Lexington and Concord, Massachusetts, many Tories, including the Jessups, feared for their fortunes. The sites of both skirmishes have long been venerated with monuments (pictured). Prints, 1800s.

The Jessups enjoyed the many economic virtues of the Hudson Valley. Land was speculated and farmed, streams were dammed for mill sites and commodities were sent back and forth from the emerging metropolis at its southern end. Print, 1800s.

the future Major Jessup, was born in 1735, the eldest of three boys. When Edward was ten years old, Joseph moved the family northwest some sixty-five miles to Dutchess County, New York, on the eastern shore of the Hudson River. The move had been prompted by grief—after his wife died, Joseph wanted his family to be close to his father, who was already established in Dutchess County.

The county's name was long thought to refer to its initial Dutch settlers, but in actuality it was a tribute by an early governor to Mary of Modena, the Duchess of York. Oddly, the formal title had originally contained the letter *t*, which was formally dropped as the English lexicon evolved by the mid-1700s. The original spelling remained as the county's name. Its population had indeed been Dutch businessmen who had seen this fertile area of the Hudson, situated midway between Albany and New York City, ideal for Indian trade. Unlike counties to the north and south, its native population was relatively benign, and combined with its abundance of produce and accessibility to river sloops, it was considered a special place to live, farm and trade. Though it grew slowly at first, it eventually prospered under the original Dutch traders and farmers who later attracted French Huguenots, German immigrants and, by the 1730s, New Englanders, who came in a wave of migration that included the Jessups.

Major Edward Jessup

This interpretation of the Bull's Head Tavern situates it by the meat yards in New York City in the eighteenth century. General George Washington knew the tavern well, even though it stood on land owned by the Jessups' Tory father-in-law. *Sketch by the author.*

The Joseph Jessup family arrived at the midsection of the Hudson known as the Long Reach, so named by Henry Hudson's crew on the *Half Moon* during its voyage of discovery a century earlier. The Jessups—father Joseph and sons Edward, Joseph and Ebenezer—soon showed that they were as well suited for commerce as were the beautiful shores and lush inlands of the Long Reach. The family began its land acquisitions with the elder Joseph's purchase of several hundred acres in the Little or Upper Nine Partner Grant north of Poughkeepsie, near Pine Plains. The area had been a speculative grant to nine partners in 1706 and was confirmed by Queen Anne in 1708. It was considered to be an enclave of established, well-bred New Yorkers.

Aspiring gentry at that time knew to marry early and well, and in 1760, Edward and his brother Ebenezer returned to Connecticut to find appropriate brides in the persons of Abigail and Elizabeth Dibble, daughters of Lieutenant Jonathan Dibble of Stamford. The lieutenant was originally from the Hamptons on the east end of Long Island and from New York (then known as York City), where he owned land on Chatham Square that he leased to the Bull's Head Tavern, an infamous public house where

George Washington was to stay just prior to his evacuation from New York in 1776. The Dibbles shared the Jessups' Tory sensibilities, and the families remained close for several decades. The Dibbles also owned land in the area of Poughkeepsie, just south of the Jessups' property near the Hudson River.

When the young couples returned to Dutchess County, the brothers showed their father's knack for business, smartly dealing in real estate acquisitions and dispositions. Edward's life was briefly interrupted at the age of thirty-five by the French and Indian War, during which he commanded a company of local militia. In the following year, 1760, grief tainted their prosperity when Sarah, Edward's daughter with Abigail, died in her first year and was buried in the Knickerbocker Cemetery in Pine Plains.

The tragedy, combined with the business boom at the northern terminus of the Hudson, prompted the families to move to Glens Falls, north of Albany. The Jessups acquired additional land from Mohawk natives and began operations on the west bank of the Hudson. The brothers owned grist- and wood mills, a ferry service and an apple tree nursery and eventually became wood operators and lumber barons, taking advantage of the ample water power source that quickly became known as Jessup's Falls. Its location a few miles to the east of nearby Glen Falls, with its stunning fifty-foot waterfall, was agreeable to their personal and professional lives. The falls was situated relatively close to the source of the Hudson, Lake Tear of the Clouds, on beautiful Mount Marcy.

According to a history of the nearby town of Queensbury written in the nineteenth century by Dr. A.W. Holden, the brothers Jessup were ardent Tory landowners who may have used questionable business practices—two traits that were not uncommon among men of affluence at the time.

> At the outbreak of the revolution...there was probably no where in this vicinity a stronger Tory nest than that existing across the west mountain... under the favour and encouragement of the brothers, Ebenezer and Edward Jessup, sharp, enterprising and apparently unscrupulous business men, who had, from time to time, secured the grant of various patents of land.

Ebenezer in particular enjoyed his riches and was described as a man of "very liberal and generous character" who, about 1770, built a log home that, according to Holden, was decorated in

> a state and style of living which bespoke opulence, taste, culture, and familiarity with the elegancies and customs of the best provincial society. If tradition is to be credited, his commodious and comfortable dwelling,

however rude may have been its exterior, was the frequent theatre of hospitable entertainments, its rooms garnished with elegant furniture, its walls embellished with costly paintings and choice engravings, its capacious tables arrayed in spotless linen and imported coven, and loaded with massive silver plate.

By the halfway point of the decade, the brothers were among the most affluent men to be found in the New York colony north of Dutchess County. But their decline began with the outbreak of Revolutionary violence 160 miles to the east in Lexington, Massachusetts, and it wasn't to end for almost a decade. Typical of the collapse of their assets was Ebenezer's rough-hewn but luxurious home: "Allot'this, with the many costly fittings and adjuncts of such a house, was at a later date plundered and carried away."

With the signing of the Declaration of Independence in the summer of 1776, few in the powerful, moneyed Tory establishment believed that George Washington's Continental army and the local Patriot militias would be a match for the vaunted British military. The Jessups, emboldened by their commercial muscle and competitive instincts, headed directly north to Crown Point on Lake Champlain to join Sir Guy Carleton's British

One of the most spectacular heritage sites in New York is found at Crown Point on Lake Champlain. A French fort was built there in 1730, blown up in 1757 and replaced by a British fort in 1759. The ruins of the barracks are surrounded by the largest defensive earthworks ever to be built in the United States. *Courtesy of Kelly Hunter.*

forces. The fort there had been controlled previously by the British, French and later the Americans, who abandoned it in 1777 for Mount Independence, situated on the east bank of the Hudson River across from Fort Ticonderoga. Afterward, British forces held the fort until the end of the Revolutionary War.

To the aloof Carleton, the brothers were bothers, their social stature falling short of their military ambition. Eighty men rallied to their cause, including their septuagenarian father Joseph, but Carleton's enthusiasm toward the local corps was restrained. He found the Jessups' nature to be pestering, so he sent them to Montreal to form part of Sir John Johnson's King's Royal Regiment. Johnson was a leading figure in northern New York whose stature, wealth, innate leadership and baronet title ensured him high military standing. While in Montreal, the Jessups' insistence that they raise their own corps confused the local commander, who thought their ambitions ran in the face of Carleton's orders. The brothers' status remained nebulous to everyone other than themselves and their men; nevertheless, they were outfitted in uniforms and continued to raise more men. According to local history, on one occasion back in New York, Edward escaped a band of Patriots by "leaping across the Hudson River."

In the lead-up to General John Burgoyne's attack on New York in 1777, various corps assembled that summer at Fort St. John on the Richelieu River just north of Lake Champlain. Meanwhile, the Jessups began mustering a corps of King's Loyal Americans near Albany, as Carleton had finally given in to their demands. Noted Loyalist historian Mary Beacock Fryer describes the sounds and sight of the flotilla of bateaux led by Burgoyne on the frigate *Royal George*, preceded by gunboats and natives, which departed for Crown Point, New York:

> *The invading army made a colourful spectacle, set against the backdrop of Green Mountains to the east and Adirondacks to the west. The British regulars and provincials were in red coats, the artillerymen in blue, as were most of the Germans (Hessians). Strains of martial music floated over the sea of boats—the brass bands of the German regiments, fifes and drums of the English and provincials, bagpipes of the Scots Highlanders.*

The brothers, named as officers—Ebenezer as a lieutenant colonel, Edward as major and Joseph as captain—brought their men to join with the British army and answer the call to battle from Crown Point. Burgoyne's initial campaign had been a success with the taking of Fort Ticonderoga, and though the action seen by the Jessups and their corps remains unclear,

Major Edward Jessup

British General John Burgoyne assembled his troops at Fort St. John on the Richelieu River, north of Lake Champlain and the American border. The fort spawned the Quebec town of Saint-Jean-sur-Richelieu. Print, 1800s.

Fryer suggests that they may have been involved in foraging and heavy action owing to the number of casualties. Ticonderoga was Burgoyne's only success of significance.

Burgoyne's next engagement was his defeat at the Battle of Freeman's Farm, after which he was unfavoured by weather and set up camp north of Saratoga. With his supplies diminished and vulnerable, he assigned the Jessups and their men the dangerous task of running supplies past rebel posts on the Hudson, an assignment carried out by Major Edward Jessup with "great zeal and attention to the orders given him for the preservation of Provision," according to a citation noted by Fryer.

His situation hopeless, Burgoyne surrendered, but not before giving the provincial corps permission to escape, an option the Jessups declined to exercise. They were subsequently taken prisoner. Eventually paroled to Montreal, the Jessups found Carleton's replacement, Sir Frederick Haldimand, no less prickly than Carleton on the matter of their commissions, but he too eventually relented. Edward Jessup saw action once more, taking part in successful raids into Lake Champlain. He was eventually promoted and saw his Jessup's Corps of King's Loyal Americans merged with Johnson's Queen's Loyal Rangers to create the Royal Rangers. Their last hostile actions during the period of 1782–83 involved scouting from Crown Point, foraging to keep

The view of Prescott from across the river at Ogdensburg, New York, shows the proximity of the two communities and the two countries. The Canadian town grew from the land grant of twelve hundred acres that Major Edward Jessup received from the Crown. Print, 1800s.

up the food supply for the army's livestock and several engineering projects for which they were commended. The hostilities ceased in April 1783, and the corps was ordered disbanded.

Over the next two years, Edward Jessup established himself with a land grant on the north shore of the St. Lawrence River, as did other men and families from New York. He and Ebenezer sailed to England in 1784 to seek compensation for their huge losses of property and possessions confiscated during the war by the Patriot courts, but they were denied in the absence of documentation.

Undaunted, Edward returned to Canada, and the village of Prescott began to grow around his grant. Cannily, he continued to acquire land just as he had done in New York in the previous decades while undertaking several new enterprises. Ebenezer stayed in London and is thought to have died there in 1789, the same year that Edward briefly returned to England. While overseas, he wisely chose not to respond to the challenge of a duel with a former Vermonter known to be an excellent swordsman and shot.

Back in Canada, Edward advanced the cause of Prescott, serving as its magistrate and later as commander of the local militia. He died there in 1816 at the age of eighty-one and is buried at a hilltop cemetery; his brother Joseph was subsequently buried beside him.

Jessup's grandson participated in the Battle of the Windmill near Prescott in 1838. Canadian rebels shared a belief with a secret American organization, the Hunters, that the Canadian administration should be replaced with a United States–style republic. The battle was brief and the attack was repelled.

Edward Jessup's son and grandson were each elected as parliamentarians in the legislature of Upper Canada, now Ontario, and both served as captains of the local militia, the latter as a captain in the Battle of the Windmill in 1838, the one of the last pro-American attempts on Canadian soil more than one hundred years after Major Edward Jessup was born.

Chapter 5

CAPTAIN SIMON FRASER

Simon Fraser of Hoosick, New York, was a toddler when his father died in a Patriot prison in Albany. Forced north from Washington County with his family, Fraser became an agile and adept explorer who scaled the Rocky Mountains and forded the wild rivers of Canada's West Coast to establish the country's first permanent white settlements beyond the great divide.

Hell's Gate in central British Columbia is a continent away—exactly three thousand miles—from Albany. It is an appropriately named topographical marvel with a 115-foot-wide channel that turns the Fraser River Canyon into a fiendish, swirling collection of stone and water, with sheer rock walls that forbid all but the most expert of climbers.

In 1808, Washington County–born, thirty-two-year-old Simon Fraser was advised to avoid the gorge's unfriendly rapids and the equally unwelcoming natives who lay in wait at its southern end. Disregarding several warnings of aboriginal mountaineers, the Canadian-raised adventurer continued into the chasm that he would later describe as "where no human beings should venture."

Fraser and two of his North West Company colleagues, aided by First Nations guides, slowly and carefully crossed makeshift scaffolds and rough-hewn bridges that hung hundreds of feet above the rock cut's foaming whirlpools. By fording this and other dangerous channels, he led an exploration considered to be among the greatest in the continent's history of settlement: the navigation of the Fraser River from its Rocky Mountain source to its mouth on the western coast of North America.

Fraser, who started life as a New Yorker of soldierly descent, was a Canadian colonial whose lineage traced back to the Scottish Highlands in

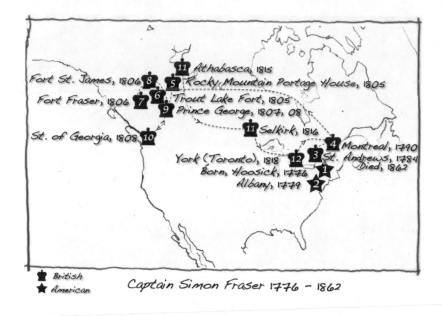

Captain Simon Fraser 1776 – 1862

Simon Fraser Sr. died in a rebel prison in Albany in 1776. Despite his accomplishments as an explorer, Simon Sr.'s son Captain Simon Fraser died indigent and crippled in the tiny village of St. Andrews a few miles north of the St. Lawrence River. *Map by the author.*

the fifteenth century. His ancestral clan, the Frasers of Lovat, took their roots from Guisachan and Culbokie in northeast Scotland; the former is known in modern times for originating the Golden Retriever dog breed and the latter, for its breathtaking scenery on the peninsula of Black Isle a few miles north of Inverness and the River Beauly.

The name Fraser likely dates back to a Norman, Pierre Fraser, who came to Scotland from France in the ninth century during the reign of King Charlemagne. Over the next few hundred years, Frasers arrived from Normandy to settle several counties, including Inverness. Sir Simon Fraser was granted lands by the Scottish king as the Lordship of Loveth, who in turn bequeathed them to Simon Fraser of Lovat.

Both men fought, as did succeeding Fraser generations, in the Scottish Wars of Independence and the Highlander clan wars. Sir Simon was said to have saved the Scottish king, Alexander III, on three different occasions, a feat acknowledged by the three crowns found on the Lovat family shield. Ultimately, however, he was captured by the British and slowly, painfully eviscerated in the same gruesome manner as his comrade in arms Sir William Wallace.

Captain Simon Fraser

Scotland's Guiscachan Estate was the ancestral home of Simon Fraser and, coincidentally, of the Golden Retriever dog breed. The first Baron of Tweedsmouth bought the three-hundred-year old Fraser property in 1854 and bred the dogs to retrieve felled grouse. *Sketch by the author.*

The Fraser clan's most notable battle came against the MacDonalds in the Battle of the Shirts in the middle of the sixteenth century in which three hundred Frasers, including William of Guisachan, were ambushed by five hundred MacDonalds in an engagement so fierce that the survivors of each clan could be counted on two hands.

By the seventeenth century, the Fraser clan was split by the fall of the House of Stuart. Those loyal to the Stuarts included the Lord Lovat of the day, who had descended from Guisachan's William Fraser VIII. He had several sons, one of whom was known as "Young Culbokie" and fought on the Highlander front lines in the Battle of Culloden, after which his ancestral home, Guisachan House, was burned to the ground. Another son, John, joined the Seventy-eighth Highlander Regiment and immigrated to North America. He eventually became a judge in Montreal. Another, Captain William Fraser—who fathered Simon the explorer—crossed the Atlantic aboard the SS *Pearl* to the colony of New York and settled in Albany in 1773.

Despite the severity of their treatment at the hands of the British after their defeat at Culloden, many transplanted Highlanders remained staunchly

Albany is the United States' oldest continuing settlement. It's charter dates back to 1686, and at the time of the American War of Independence, it was the colonies' most populous county. Print, 1800s.

loyal to King George III from the outset of the American Revolution. Fraser's arrival coincided with the rise of Yankee unrest in response to Britain's Stamp and Tea Acts that culminated with the Boston Tea Party in December of that year.

Captain Fraser had ten children, the youngest of whom was Simon, born in May 1776 in Hoosick, New York, just across the colonial border from Bennington, Vermont. The American Revolution ignited at the time of his birth: Virginia had drafted and accepted its Declaration of Rights, France had decided to aid the Americans against the British and General John Burgoyne had arrived in Canada in anticipation of all-out war.

The following summer was the crisis point for most Loyalist families when rebel forces scored victories over the British at Hubbardton and Bennington. Simon Fraser Sr. was captured, taken to Albany and placed in jail. His health and the fortunes of Loyalists diminished over the next three years as Patriot momentum became irreversible. His wife and family, with their livestock and most other possessions gone, managed to hold fast and keep their property with help of other Loyalist families and a few sympathetic friends among the rebels.

Captain Fraser died in prison in Albany in 1779, and five years later his widow sold their farm and escaped with her children to Canada, initially living west of Montreal at Coteau-du-Lac on the north shore of the St.

Fatality rates in American and British prisons were high for reasons particular to each side in the conflict. The rebels had less experience with the rules of war; the British deliberately kept prison conditions poor to intimidate rebels and encourage enlistment. *Sketch by the author.*

Lawrence. Later, they settled at St. Andrews near modern-day Cornwall. Unlike the scattered north shore settlements, Montreal was bustling with the rising fortunes of the fur trade as the inland and overseas shipping upon which it was dependent grew less hindered by war.

The Canadian colonies' Hudson's Bay Company was at the heart of the action, with its century-long stranglehold on a network of fur trappers and traders across the western half of the continent. Ambitious Highlanders such as Simon Fraser's uncle John, the Montreal judge, saw an opportunity to challenge the domination of the "company of adventurers" with their recently formed North West Company. John Fraser arranged for Simon to join him in 1790 in Montreal, where he learned the ways of commerce while dealing with French Canadian voyageurs and rubbing elbows within the Scottish and English gentility. Simon eventually headed to the northwestern wilderness and apprenticed in the company's Athabasca department until the turn of the century. In 1801, he graduated to full partnership.

Montreal was the gateway to Canada's west in the eighteenth and nineteenth centuries. It served as headquarters for Fraser's North West Company and its rival, the Hudson's Bay Company. Print, 1800s.

Captain Simon Fraser

In becoming a "Nor'wester" at the age of twenty-five, Simon Fraser was in good company. Simon McTavish, the son of a Highlander who fought in the French and Indian War, was a shrewd and cagey Montreal entrepreneur who managed to gain control of the company at the age of thirty-seven by building his fortune on commissions from the sale of furs and rum. McTavish was joined by James McGill, another Scotsman who was parsimonious in life but generous in death. McGill bequeathed his property and a large sum to the university that has borne his name for almost two hundred years.

This collection of clever Scotsmen combined their capital with the knowledge of the French inland traders to push into the Lake Athabasca and Mackenzie River regions. Years before Fraser's arrival, a Connecticut Yankee by the name of Peter Pond mapped the northwestern reaches of the continent as the Revolutionary War got underway. Pond was a bold Nor'wester whose aggressive nature led to his mapping of the Athabasca and Great Slave Lake areas but also to his involvement in two separate violent incidents in which two of his colleagues were murdered. In one of the killings, Pond was known to be the triggerman.

Another forerunner of Fraser's by about a dozen years was Nor'wester partner Sir Alexander Mackenzie, who blazed a trail west of the Rockies to the Pacific coast via the Bella Coola River, a route that did not prove commercially viable. Nevertheless, Mackenzie was the first European north of Mexico to reach the Pacific overland. In 1805, with the benefit of the early work of these and other forerunners, Simon Fraser was given the assignment of establishing trading posts west of the Rockies, laying claim to the region and finding more practical routes to the coast than those Mackenzie had found.

Fraser set out in earnest and began with crossing the Rocky Mountains. The first trading post he established that autumn was Rocky Mountain Portage House, now Hudson's Hope, along the Peace River on the mountain range's western slope. That winter he established Trout Lake Fort, now Fort McLeod, and in so doing created modern Canada's first permanent European settlement west of the Continental Divide. With his Scottish lineage never far from his mind, Fraser named the hilly woodlands New Caledonia, the Latin name originally given to Scotland in Roman antiquity.

In rapid succession, and with the help of his colleagues James McDougall and James Stuart, Fraser established the lucrative trading posts Forts Fraser and St. James in 1806. The following spring, Fraser came to believe that he could navigate to the Columbia River and the Pacific coast via a series of rivers, including the one that now bears his name. A local famine and a shortage of supplies prevented him from embarking on the trek in 1807, but

Gold was discovered near the Fraser River fifty years after Simon Fraser's explorations. The Fraser Canyon Gold Rush eventually led to white settlement and the formation of British Columbia.

in the interim he established another fort at the location of the modern city of Prince George. From there, he began his pursuit of his Pacific quest in May 1808.

Within two weeks of setting out, Fraser and his large contingent of two-dozen voyageurs, native scouts and colleagues James Stuart and Jules Quesnel were forced to give up their canoes when they encountered the river's "big" canyon and its fierce sub-canyons with narrow gorges of boiling rapids and steep, impossibly high rock cliffs. Aboriginal guides whose tribes had feasted on the river's plentiful fish and treaded its dangerous edges for millennia led Fraser and his men through passageways and over primitive scaffolding and crossings in a dangerous, lengthy portage.

The party continued using borrowed canoes once clear of the canyon and followed the river all the way to its mouth at the Strait of Georgia and the site of modern-day Vancouver. But hostility between the Musqueam and the Kwantlen tribes, descendant branches of the West Coast Salish peoples, led to an extremely dangerous arrival and departure for the heroic explorer and his team.

En route, Fraser had met the Kwantlens, a tribe who had never before encountered white men or their odd possessions. Calling them the "Sky" people, the chief had promised the whites a canoe but reneged the following day when a dust-up broke out after some young Kwantlens stole some of their camp items. Following a shoving match, Fraser feigned an angry outburst, commandeered the canoe and headed downriver without the benefit of a native scout.

They were met by angry Musqueams at the other end who viewed the unannounced arrival of Fraser's party as hostile. Fraser had recklessly come ashore to take in the wonder of the Pacific Ocean strait and the natives' fifteen-hundred-foot-long tribal house when he immediately encountered warriors brandishing clubs. Fraser's party was quickly surrounded as Kwantlens closed in from the rear. With their weapons loaded, raised and threatening, Fraser and his men withdrew to deeper water and headed back upriver.

Fraser and his men paddled upriver for the entire night with the natives in close pursuit. Exhausted, they encountered more resistance from tribes that had been friendly during their descent of the river but had turned hostile once encouraged by the Musqueams and Kwantlens. Four days after their

The Kwantlen First Nation villages are located on the south bank of the Fraser River near Fort Langley. The Musqueam peoples are of the marshy lowlands in the southwest corner of the modern city of Vancouver.

escape, Fraser and his team had to fight once more when an angry tribe tried to steal their canoe. Forced back downstream over rapids that caused several near-drownings, Fraser later estimated that they had eluded as many as seven hundred warring natives.

By the time Fraser arrived back at Fort George on August 6, 1808, he had to overcome another hostile native engagement that drove his men to near-mutiny—they wanted to abandon the river and flee overland. The men were hungry, fatigued and unnerved by the unrelenting pursuit of the natives, yet Fraser was able to restore their morale by having them swear an oath of loyalty and change into their finest attire. The natives, evidently impressed by the men's return to good form, retreated. Fraser's personal morale, however, had been struck down by serious injury and by his realization midway in his exploration that the river he had conquered was not the Columbia. Despite his ordeals and accomplishments, Fraser and his business partners did not consider the arduous journey a success.

Fraser's career continued and he ran the Mackenzie River Department for several years. By 1815, he was determined to retire from his life as a Nor'wester but agreed to serve one more year in Athabasca, despite increasing hostilities between his own company, the Hudson's Bay Company, the French-Indian métis and newly arrived settlers.

The fifth Earl of Selkirk, a Hudson's Bay Company shareholder, had established a colony at Red River in the middle of the métis' buffalo hunting grounds. At stake was the supply of pemmican, a provision made from buffalo meat and fat on which Nor'westers had relied for decades as sustenance during their fur trading trips. The new settlers needed it too, and when their leaders tried to prohibit its sale to the fur traders, the métis formed a militia. The rivalries led to a gunfight in 1816 known as the Battle of Seven Oaks, in which settlers tried to block the métis from selling pemmican to the Nor'westers and lost twenty of their men in the process.

Métis leaders and North West Company partners, including Simon Fraser, were charged by Lord Selkirk with complicity in the deaths and were tried but acquitted in 1818 in York, the site of present-day Toronto. At this time, Fraser retired and returned to St. Andrews near the St. Lawrence River and Cornwall, Ontario, where his mother had originally settled nearly four decades earlier. In 1820, he married and began leading a quiet and happily uneventful life of farming and operating mills.

During the next year, the name of the company to which he had devoted two decades of his life all but disappeared when the British government forced the merger of the North West Company with Hudson's Bay Company. The unproductive feuding between the two companies was finally put to an end.

Captain Simon Fraser

The Hudson's Bay Company makes the following claim: "Canada's Merchants Since 1670." Indeed, the company is the oldest commercial corporation in North America and among the oldest in the world.

In 1822, Fraser became a captain in the Stormont militia and was called into action during the Rebellion of 1837, in which he suffered a significant, crippling injury. In his addled condition, he couldn't operate his farm and mills and lived the rest of his days on a small pension. He died in poverty in 1862. He had been made aware the year before that the river that bore his name was deeply attached to the Klondike Gold Rush and key to many men's fortunes. In a further irony, the great-grandson of his cousin William Fraser IX—"Young Culbokie"—sold Guisachan, the clan's ancestral estate in the Highlands of Scotland, to the family of Lady Aberdeen, wife of Lord Aberdeen, who was appointed governor general of Canada in 1893.

In 1891, the viceregal couple purchased the Coldstream Ranch in the Okanagan Valley of British Columbia, the province whose first settlement was established by Fraser. They renamed the property Guisachan, and the main building still stands in 2009, one year after the 200th anniversary of Simon Fraser's great adventure.

Chapter 6

CAPTAIN JOHN DESERONTYON

Aptly named Odeserundiye—"where thunder was"—Captain John Deserontyon stood alongside the great Mohawk leaders of his time. A fierce native Loyalist, he left New York's Mohawk Valley in ashes and spent his final days near his namesake town, Deseronto, at the junction of the St. Lawrence River and Lake Ontario.

T he smell of gunpowder had faded, and a long-awaited calm was befalling the Mohawk Valley by 1783. The Revolutionary War had ended, and the Mohawk natives of western New York had been exiled to the north, to Canada. Many made brief, violent returns to burn the crops and villages that populated the valley that had once been their homeland. Such bitter acts left many white farmers and their families dead and ensured that any Mohawk who dared enter the valley again would face equally fierce retribution.

Despite the dangers, a Mohawk party silently entered the river's corridor that year on a secret mission. It avoided the scattered remnants of the American "long knives," as the rebel army was known, and made its way toward Fort Hunter, near the site of modern-day Amsterdam. The party's assignment was to recover an invaluable symbol of Mohawk dignity—it was to retrieve the Queen Anne silver that had been hidden and buried six years earlier on the farm of Boyd Hunter.

The silver had been given to the four native kings who had traveled to meet with the British sovereign in 1710. Queen Anne gifted the royal silver to the chiefs, who passed it down through several tribal generations as a symbol of England's and the church's devotion to the Mohawk nation. Decades later, the natives buried their treasure near the chapel at Fort Hunter before they made their escape to Canada in 1777.

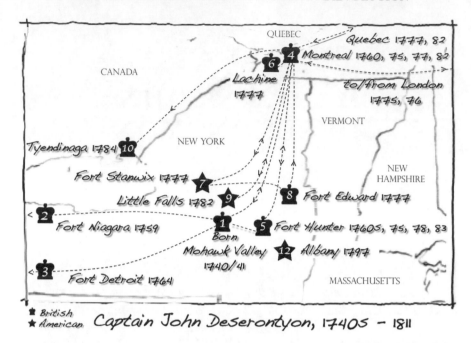

QUEBEC
Quebec 1777, 82
Montreal 1760, 75, 77, 82
CANADA
Lachine 1777
to/from London 1775, 76
VERMONT
Tyendinaga 1784 ⑩
NEW YORK
NEW HAMPSHIRE
Fort Stanwix 1777 ★⑦
Little Falls 1782 ★⑨
⑧ Fort Edward 1777
⑧ ❷
Fort Niagara 1759
❶ Born
⑤ Fort Hunter 1760S, 75, 78, 83
Mohawk Valley ★⑫ Albany 1797
1740/41
❸
Fort Detroit 1764
MASSACHUSETTS

♚ British
★ American   Captain John Deserontyon, 1740S – 1811

Captain John Deserontyon, a resourceful and resilient native chief from New York's Mohawk Valley (1), fought gamely during the Revolutionary War and eventually resettled many Mohawks to Canada on Lake Ontario's Bay of Quinte (10). *Map by the author.*

Leading the secret mission was Captain John Deserontyon, a youthful veteran of the British army who had heard the clap of cannonades and gunfire from a very young age. Fittingly, Deserontyon's Mohawk name was *Odeserundiye*, which translated to "where thunder was."

Deserontyon was born in the Mohawk Valley in the 1740s. Little is known of his early years, other than his participation in the siege of Fort Niagara in 1759 as a teenager. Fort Niagara was built in the second half of the seventeenth century and was expanded and fortified in 1755 during the French and Indian War. During the summer of 1759—two months before Quebec fell to General Wolfe—the British, led by Brigadier General John Prideaux, placed Fort Niagara under siege. Prideaux lost his head, literally, when he was decapitated by a British mortar being test fired in the British camp.

To the New York militia and John Deserontyon, the siege was a coming-of-age engagement in which its ambitious and gifted leader, Sir William Johnson, stepped forward to replace Prideaux. Johnson had received his baronetcy four years earlier after the Battle of Lake George, where he lost his good friend and Mohawk leader King Hendrick. The chief had traveled

Captain John Deserontyon

A communion set was given to the "Four Iroquois Kings" by Queen Anne during their visit to England in 1710. It was buried on a farm near Fort Hunter in 1777 to protect it from approaching rebels. *Sketch by the author.*

with others of the Wolf, Bear and Turtle Clans as three of the four "Iroquois" kings to receive Queen Anne's silver in London in 1710. The fourth sachem was not Iroquoian but was in fact Mohican.

Johnson's baronet status afforded him huge land tracts upon which he built several large estates; his lands and his large extended family played significant roles in the course of his life. The year after he took Fort Niagara, Johnson joined Sir Jeffery Amherst at Montreal for the final defeat of the French in 1760, a battle at which Deserontyon was also present as a teenager. Johnson carried with him the title of "Sole Agent and Superintendent of Indians and Their Affairs" and had assembled more than six hundred Iroquois to assist in his campaign. Deserontyon was witnessing the very finest in colonial leadership and compassion as Johnson saw to it that his prisoners were properly shod and clothed for their long journeys while in captivity.

Less compassionate was Sir Jeffery Amherst, whose impeccable military reputation was tarnished by his correspondence supporting the use of "biological warfare" during the Pontiac Rebellion of 1763, in which Deserontyon also saw action. Pontiac was an Ottawa chief with French sympathies who led an uprising against the British after the French governor general, Marquis de Vaudreuil, surrendered Quebec. The Native Americans had enjoyed prosperous trade with the French and were angered by Amherst's decision to discontinue the custom of providing them gifts in exchange for their friendship and assistance. Amherst's indifference was evident in his writings, in which he suggested blankets riddled with smallpox be distributed to the natives as a way of helping put down the rebellion.

Johnson initiated parlays with Pontiac and did so with the help of his Iroquois circle, which included Deserontyon and other Mohawk leaders, most of whom had helped tutor Sir William's son and nephew Guy in their culture and art of negotiation. Pontiac had persuaded the Chippewas, Delawares, Shawnees and Senecas to attack British forts with a viciousness uncharacteristic even for frontier war that resulted in many whites being brutally killed or captured. To bring an end to the bloodshed, Johnson and his entourage held peace settlement discussions with the Six Nations during 1763, and the following year they held a parlay with fourteen hundred natives at Fort Niagara.

John Deserontyon helped guard white settlers from Seneca attacks, and then, in 1764, he went to Detroit to impose peace on the Delawares and Shawnees. He joined Colonel John Bradstreet and General Israel Putnam on an expedition from Fort Niagara, on the eastern edge of Lake Erie, to Fort

Captain John Deserontyon

This interpretation of Fort Hunter shows its twelve-foot palisade and two of its blockhouses. Built in 1711, it was torn down in 1820 during the construction of the original Erie Canal. *Sketch by the author.*

Detroit, where they successfully put down residual native violence in the area, retrieved captives and managed the peace once the rebellion ended.

By this time, Deserontyon had already become a Mohawk chief at the British settlement of Fort Hunter. The fortification known as the Lower Canajoharie Castle was related to the four native leaders' visit to England half a century earlier, which had been sponsored by Peter Schuyler, then mayor of Albany, who wanted to raise awareness in the royal court of the need for a greater military presence in the colonies. One result of their earnest trip was greater resolve by British missionaries to convert the natives to Christianity.

The Society for the Propagation of the Gospel in Foreign Parts ordered that a fort with a chapel and a mission house be built along the Mohawk River at its junction with the Schoharie River. The Queen Anne silver was a communion set intended for use during Anglican masses held at the settlement. The garrison was named Fort Hunter to honor the colonial governor.

The fort was built as a square with a twelve-foot-high wooden palisade and two-story blockhouses at each corner housing seven- and nine-pounder cannons. The first chapel, built in 1711, was a log cabin—a modest home for royal silver—and was replaced by a stone chapel in the 1740s, about the time John Deserontyon was born. By the 1770s, just prior to the outbreak of war, Sir William Johnson built a school in the fort and rebuilt the chapel with a new floor, pulpit, communion table, belfry and bell. Eventually, two services were held every Sunday in the chapel, one for the Mohawk converts and one for the white settlers. The fort, however, suffered a fire in 1773 and lost a blockhouse and two of its walls.

The fort's parsonage was built one mile east, and it was there that Mohawk leader Joseph Brant translated the Anglican Book of Common Prayer into the Iroquois language. When war broke out, Deserontyon was garrisoned and Fort Hunter became part of a British network of fortifications running the length of the valley. Sir William Johnson died from a stroke in 1774, and the management of his estates and the militia fell to his son John, while his nephew, Guy Johnson, managed Indian affairs. Both men headed units of New York's Tyron County militia. Joseph Brant, a confidant of Deserontyon's, served as Johnson's secretary in his role as superintendent of Indian affairs.

In the spring of 1775, the Patriot Committee of Safety issued a reprimand to Guy Johnson for his "aggressive and partisan acts." With this order, the Patriots cleverly shunted the Johnsons from their militia commands. Guy was forced to move up the Mohawk Valley to the German Flats using the ruse that he was calling another Indian parlay. From there, he escaped to Canada along with Joseph Brant, 30 other Mohawks and 120 settlers.

Deserontyon joined them but first ensured that the Queen Anne silver was buried and hidden from Patriot view. In going to Canada, he left behind all he owned: a substantial house, more than eighty acres of rich, arable farmland and all of its accompanying tools and equipment, plus a collection of personal possessions equal in value to his farm.

The next year, Deserontyon returned to the aid of Sir John Johnson, who had dug in at his estate with many of his Loyalist tenants; together, they faced down constant threats from the rebels. Eventually, Congress ordered American general Philip Schuyler to march with as many men as he could muster to disarm them. He arrested Johnson in January 1776, and Johnson was released on parole on his word that he would cease forming Loyalist militias.

The previous few months had not been good ones for the British war effort. Sorel, Montreal and Trois-Rivières had fallen to the rebels, and several Continental army units under Generals Richard Montgomery and Benedict Arnold had laid siege to Quebec. On New Year's Eve 1775, the rebel attack on Quebec failed when twelve hundred men, including British regulars, sailors, Canadians and Royal Highlanders, effectively saved the province. The winter-long siege of Quebec, however, continued into May 1776.

That same month, Deserontyon and his scouts heard of the Continental army's preparations to again attack Johnson Hall and put an end to Johnson's continued arming of his Loyalist tenants despite the terms of his parole. The rebels had been recently heartened by the battles in Lexington and

Captain John Deserontyon

Deserontyon and Joseph Brant met with Sir Frederick Haldimand in Quebec City in 1783. They had strongly protested the Treaty of Paris, in which the lands below the forty-ninth parallel were ceded to the victorious Americans. Print, 1700s.

Concord, Massachusetts, and Congress had issued orders instructing the thirteen colonies to form their own governments. Emboldened, General Philip Schuyler dispatched Colonel Elias Dayton with three hundred men to arrest Johnson just as Deserontyon sent word that the rebels were en route.

Johnson prepared to escape to Canada while Deserontyon and other Mohawk leaders delayed Dayton with protracted negotiations before allowing his troops to cross their lands. This gave Sir John enough time to gather Mohawk guides and approximately 170 tenants and set off across the Appalachians for Canada. The trip was much harsher than expected, and the party eventually had to eat plants, such as wild onions and any other marginally edible vegetation, simply to stay alive. Despite arriving at the St. Lawrence River exhausted and close to death, he and his men took to the pursuit of retreating rebel attackers who managed to escape.

Meanwhile, Deserontyon, Guy Johnson, Joseph Brant and a fourth Tory named Gilbert Tice had gone to England but were unsuccessful in securing official authority to negotiate on behalf of the Iroquois and returned to Montreal via New York.

During the next twelve months, the British Americans and their native allies prepared to attack western New York. John Johnson had formed battalions of the King's Royal Yorkers and had proposed a venture back into

The Tyron County militia under Brigadier General Nicholas Herkimer was ambushed in the Battle of Oriskany a few miles east of Fort Stanwix, in modern-day Rome, New York. Print, 1800s.

the Mohawk Valley that fit well within the British strategy of cutting New England off from the rest of the colonies with an attack down the Hudson River Valley and a push north by loyal forces from New York City.

Deserontyon had gone to Quebec City in the spring of 1777; he met with General John Burgoyne and learned of a planned assault on Fort Stanwix near modern-day Rome. Prior to Colonel Barry St. Leger's arrival in New York, Deserontyon had received orders to lead a scouting party back into the valley and assess rebel defenses at the fort.

He came within three-quarters of a mile of the fort that July, and according to historians Gavin Watt and James Morrison, "Deserontyon's men surprised a 16-man work party...five men were captured, four scalps taken and one of the dead men was left 'shockingly butchered.'"

Deserontyon returned from the skirmish with prisoners, whose interrogation revealed that, among other things, the garrison at Fort Stanwix was well aware of the planned assault.

St. Leger largely ignored the intelligence from Deserontyon's captives and proceeded with his assault as planned; it failed, and he was forced to place the fort under siege. Joseph Brant's sister, Sir William Johnson's native widow, Molly Brant, alerted St. Leger to the approach of an American relief force under General Nicholas Herkimer from the east. St. Leger dispatched Brant, Sir John Johnson, Deserontyon, other Mohawk warriors and Royal Yorkers to ambush Herkimer. They successfully did so; Herkimer was wounded and later died, but St. Leger's siege ultimately failed.

When American troops scoured the evacuated British camp, a surprised Deserontyon was fired upon by an American soldier. According to Watt and Morrison, "The buckshot caught John Deserontyon full in the meat of his left arm and breast and he crashed to the floor." His wounds were serious but not fatal. He headed east and gathered several Mohawk families from Fort Hunter before it was sacked by Patriots. Deserontyon was wounded a second time when he and his party had to fight through a transplanted New Hampshire regiment. Afterward, angry rebels sacked Fort Hunter, and Queen Anne's chapel was defiled and used by the rebels as a tavern and stable. A frustrated Deserontyon, meanwhile, headed north to Lachine.

The next year, 1778, Deserontyon returned to the valley from Canada via the Appalachians to retrieve and rescue remaining Mohawks and Loyalists who were left in the Fort Hunter area. At the same time, he captured more rebels and burned homes. Over the next several years, he participated in raids into the Mohawk Valley, in which countless buildings were burned, farms destroyed and rebels scalped. Particularly violent were the attacks led by Sir John Johnson that began in the west at Oswego and moved east as far as Fort Hunter. Deserontyon's final raid took place in 1782, when he destroyed a mill at Little Falls and took more prisoners. The white population in the valley had dropped from ten thousand in 1777 to three thousand in 1783, largely due to the Loyalist departures and British retaliations.

The Mohawk had supported the British throughout the war, largely on Sir Guy Carleton's and his successor Sir Frederick Haldimand's promises to restore their ancestral homelands. Joseph Brant and John Deserontyon were livid with the British for ordering an end to the fighting in 1782 and ceding the lands south of the forty-ninth parallel in the Treaty of Versailles the following year. Brant and Deserontyon decided to travel to Quebec to meet with Haldimand. They stridently pointed out that the Mohawks had been free and independent prior to the war and that the British had no right to negotiate away their land to the Americans.

Haldimand could offer them no recourse other than land that the British had bought from the Mississauga tribe. In May 1783, Brant and Deserontyon accompanied surveyors to inspect the St. Lawrence front where it joined Lake Ontario, near the mouth of the Salmon River. Deserontyon had

The first house in Canajoharie, built by Martin J. Van Alstyne before 1749, was the scene of Brigadier General Nicholas Herkimer's commissioning in 1775. The extended Alstyne family included both Patriots and Tories. *Keepsake scan, author's collection.*

finally led the secret mission into the Mohawk Valley to recover the Queen Anne silver that year and was happy with Haldimand's offer of ninety-two thousand acres at the Bay of Quinte; in part, because it was the birthplace of Deganawida, the "Great Peacemaker," who had provided the inspiration

OUSE - 1749
OLONIAL DAYS. SCENE OF MANY
HE REVOLUTION.

of the Iroquois Confederacy with Chief Hiawatha many centuries earlier. Brant chose a land grant much farther west along the Grand River in order to accommodate the Senecas' need to be closer to their homeland.

The following year, Deserontyon brought twenty Mohawk families from their temporary settlement in Lachine, near modern-day Kahnawake, where they had lived for five years, to settle the area known as Tyendinaga (derived from Joseph Brant's native name *Thayendanegea*) at Quinte. They did so a month before the white Loyalists arrived nearby. The natives began building farmhouses, clearing the lands, sowing crops and rearing horses and livestock, but over the years the amount of acreage owned by the Mohawks dwindled through disputes with the Crown.

Deserontyon had spurned Brant's invitation to build a unified community by the Grand River because he felt it was too close for comfort to the victorious Americans. According to historian Janice Potter-MacKinnon, Deserontyon wrote, "I thought I could not live in peace so near those people... the Americans are like a worm that cuts off corn as soon as it appears." Deserontyon, who had married Joseph Brant's daughter Catherine, built a chapel and a Christian schoolhouse for his followers and his own children. Over time, his relations with Brant grew uneasy, as his father-in-law accused him of causing divisions within the Mohawk nation. For his war losses, Deserontyon received £800 as a lump sum and £45 annually as a pension, in addition to three thousand acres of land. In 1797, he and Joseph Brant sought closure by going to New York and agreeing to withdraw Mohawk land claims in return for a small sum.

In 1798, King George III designated Deserontyon's little wooden church as a "Chapel Royale" and gave the Mohawks a three-paneled alter piece

White and Mohawk Loyalists settled on Lake Ontario's north shore by the Bay of Quinte, led by Major Peter van Alstyne and Captain John Deserontyon, respectively. Print, 1800s.

with commandments and prayers translated into their language. The church bell he donated is considered to be the first in Upper Canada, now Southern Ontario.

The eight pieces of Queen Anne silver, which Deserontyon retrieved from Fort Hunter in 1777, had been missing a chalice at the time of its recovery. The remaining seven pieces were divided: four went to Brant's community and three to Deserontyon's for use in its chapel. Appropriately, the silver was used during Deserontyon's funeral after he died in 1811.

The British Crown continued its largess to Deserontyon's chapel with a gift of a Bible from Queen Victoria when the wooden building was replaced by a stone church in the 1840s. During a royal visit in 1984, Queen Elizabeth II presented the Bay of Quinte Mohawks with a replacement chalice for the one that had gone missing two centuries earlier. This piece and the silver recovered by Deserontyon in 1777 are used in official ceremonies on the Tyendinaga Mohawk Territory to this day.

Chapter 7

LIEUTENANT HENRY SIMMONS

Lieutenant Henry Simmons was one of thousands of British soldiers and Loyalists displaced by the Revolutionary War. His journal of 1777 and 1778 tells how he and his forty-five men overcame their loss to the Patriots and eventually established their new homes along the north shore of the St. Lawrence River.

The Hudson River Valley twists a three-hundred-mile path south from Lake Champlain to the metropolis of New York and into the Atlantic Ocean. Henry Hudson lent the river his name after he sailed into its mouth onboard the *Half Moon* with a crew of British and Dutch seamen in 1609. That same year, Samuel de Champlain followed the Richelieu River south from the St. Lawrence River to the lake that would bear his name.

In the hundreds of years since, the two river valleys and their adjoining lake (they were joined by canal in 1823) have helped shape the early military and cultural history of North America. For the United States, the waterways were tools to trap and defeat the British during their War of Independence; for Canada, they provided Loyalists an escape route from American retribution and a pathway to a new home.

The New England rebels of the late 1770s used their Committees of Safety as instruments of war, though often their motivation was personal gain. Loyalists were evicted and banished from towns or homes that their families had either owned or leased for generations. One such town was Claverack on the east bank of the lower Hudson Valley, where Lieutenant Henry Simmons lived and prospered. He left in August 1777 to defend the Crown against Patriot forces and never returned. Eight years passed before he finally received his land grants and led four hundred British veterans and families along the Canadian bank of the St. Lawrence River from Quebec to just west of Kingston.

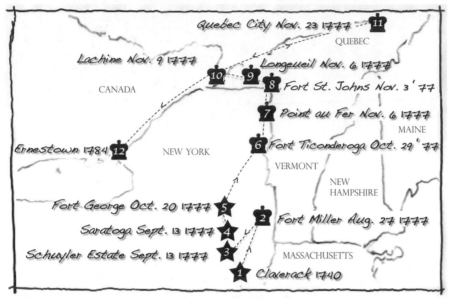

Lt. Henry Simmons, 1740 – 1816

Lieutenant Henry Simmons was born at Claverlack Landing (1) in the Hudson Valley in 1740. He entered the Revolutionary War in 1777. His service was shortened by the Continental army victory at Saratoga (4) in October of that year. *Map by the author.*

Simmons's handwritten journal for the two years between his departure from Claverack and his arrival in Quebec reveal the fortunes—both good and bad—encountered by Loyalist soldiers on their way to building new lives in Canada.

The Simmons saga began when his parents arrived from Prussia and settled in Theerbos, near the settlement of Claverack, New York, early in the eighteenth century. The colony was named Claverack Landing and was surrounded by lands purchased by the Dutch from the Mohican Indians in 1662. To the Dutch, who worked the fields and farms of Claverack, and the nearby city of Hudson, the village provided sustenance; to New England mariners, Claverack became an inland seaport for shipping and processing whale oil. The town was located on the reach between Storm King Mountain and Hudson, 150 miles upriver from New York City. The whalers and merchants who had come down from Cape Cod, Martha's Vineyard and Nantucket helped Claverack grow into a substantial port town by the early 1700s.

Henry Simmons was born there in 1740, christened Henrick Simon; he became anglicized and lived peaceably in the lower Hudson Valley well

Lieutenant Henry Simmons

The services of thirty thousand soldiers from Hesse Cassel, Brunswick and elsewhere in Germany were purchased from Frederick II by his uncle King George III. Not all the soldiers joined the force voluntarily. Print, 1800s.

into his fourth decade. By the mid-1770s, American Patriots were in open rebellion, and family patriarchs were pressured to declare themselves either Tories loyal to the Crown or American Patriots willing to raise arms against the British.

Americans attempted to capture Quebec and managed to hold the city under siege for the winter of 1775. They were forced to retreat the following spring when the British fleet arrived, enabling General Guy Carleton to begin a counterattack a few months later. By the end of the year, Carleton had driven the rebels south and gained control of Lake Champlain at Crown Point, the largest military fort in North America at the time. In the spring of 1777, he was replaced by General John Burgoyne, who began the march of the British army, buttressed by Hessians, down along the shores of the lake toward Albany, the northernmost political and commercial center in the Hudson Valley.

American Tories suffered greatly during this time. Henry Simmons was among them, and in August 1777 he began to keep a journal in which he wrote of his hasty departure from Claverack. His harried prose and colonial vernacular reflected the spirit of his times:

The Sixteeth Day of August, 1777, I left my house at Claverack and Sat out with a Compiny of Seven and twenty Men and officers to go to General Burguins armey Which was at the time at Fort Miller.

According to the transcription and interpretation of Simmons's longhand journal by Dr. H.C. Burleigh, an erudite twentieth-century member of the United Empire Loyalists of Canada, the men had traveled "75 miles in 11 days…through enemy country, likely at night along untrodden paths, fording streams, and hiding in thickets by day. Their food was what they could carry on their backs."

According to Burleigh, Simmons described his arrival at the Battenkill River and his enlistment in the British army: "Arifet at the Butten Kill in the flyeing arme the 27th of augt and Was musterct that Same Day and Joint Lt. Co. Je Saups till further ourder aid there we Lay till the 1st of Septr."

Henry Simmons had signed on under commander Lieutenant Colonel Edward Jessup. Jessup was born in the Hudson Valley and had become familiar with the lands around Lake Champlain while serving with the British during the French and Indian War under General Jeffery Amherst in 1759.

Jessup had been awarded half a million acres in the Adirondack Mountains for his military service, and he and his brother established a community northwest of Albany that they named Jessup's Landing. By 1776, they had joined the regiment of Sir John Johnson, one of the largest landowners in New York. Edward was later given command of a roll-up corps of all of Governor Haldimand's troops, the Loyal Rangers.

At the time that Simmons enlisted, Jessup's regiment was in pursuit of about twenty-five hundred American soldiers who were in retreat from Fort Ticonderoga. The Americans pulled back across Lake Champlain and headed into Vermont just as the British were taking the fort. Burgoyne ordered their pursuit, but his men were surprised by a rear guard action by the local rebel militia, the Green Mountain Boys, who engaged and defeated them at Hubbardton.

By then, Henry Simmons was a lieutenant in the Loyal Rangers and was commanded by a Hessian officer, Captain Christian Wehr. Simmons described ordering two men back to Claverlack for more men and arms and the false alarm that they experienced soon afterward: "Chrichtyan havver… Went home to gitt more men…the 8th Sept we get arms for 12 men and thath nigh we was Alarrmet as if the enemy were coming But it Wa a fals Larm."

The British army, including Jessup's regiment, continued its pursuit of the Americans and arrived at Fort Miller after the Americans had departed.

Lieutenant Henry Simmons

General Philip Schuyler of Albany was a seminal figure of the Northern Department of the Continental Army. As a civilian, his property holdings were extensive. Simmons noted one of these properties in his diary en route to Saratoga. Print, 1800s.

The tattered Continental army was proving resilient, had been regrouped and reorganized by General Phillip Schuyler and, under the command of Horatio Gates, had left for Saratoga, New York. According to Simmons's journal, his detachment arrived at Schuyler's estate on "the 10th we gat armes for 9 men more [and by the 13th of September] we…as fare as Shullers upper Sawmill."

The British army had started its march from Canada with 3,000 British regulars, 4,000 German Hessians and 650 Canadians and Indians, and along the way it added Loyalists from New York and Vermont. After their defeat at Hubbardton, the British suffered a more significant loss at Bennington, Vermont, when a large force of Hessians was ordered by Burgoyne to attack the town and raid its storage depot but was repulsed and took heavy casualties.

By the time the British army arrived at Saratoga, its size had been significantly reduced. Its arduous land push from the east bank of the Hudson had left it fatigued and depleted of supplies, in sharp contrast to the Americans who had been ordered reinforced by General George Washington. His most aggressive general, Benedict Arnold, arrived from the south; General Israel Putnam came from the north, along with reinforcements from Massachusetts, riflemen from Virginia and militia from all over New England.

The first battle of Saratoga was on Freeman's Farm on September 19, and Henry Simmons described its outcome in his journal:

> And their We lay until the 19th till some time in the night and…that Day our Flying Arme and the Rebels had a Battle at free mans farme But our men Boit the Rebels to Reterin and Kilt betwin 3 and 4 hundaert of the Enmy and we had about two hundred Deat and Wountet.

Three days later, and less than two weeks before the second and final battle of Saratoga, Simmons's two men returned from Claverack with reinforcements for his detachment and a prisoner they had taken en route: "Haver and Hess Came in agin and Brought 18 men with them and A Commetee man PreSsoner."

By this time, Simmons's detachment consisted of forty-five men. It was engaged in the Second Battle of Saratoga, known as the Battle of Bemis Heights, in which the rebels held firm and forced the British into retreat: "And other Batle West of fremens…on the hill and that Day Engaget with Canons But how many was killet at eithere Sit I can not say."

Afterward, the British attempted to retreat across to the west bank of the Hudson but were blocked by Gates and forced to march back toward the east and encamp on a hill north of the "Fish Kill" and Saratoga. Burgoyne's

Lieutenant Henry Simmons

In his diary, Lieutenant Henry Simmons described the extensive British casualties as "about two hundred Deat and Wountet" at the Battle of Freemans Farm. General Benedict Arnold (pictured) was wounded in the subsequent Battle of Bemis Heights. Print, 1800s.

army was weakened, wounded and surrounded, and on October 17, 1777, he and his troops met General Horatio Gates at Saratoga and surrendered. Lieutenant Henry Simmons and his men were among the fifty-eight hundred men of the British army who lay down their arms that day:

> *The Sam Day we wend as fare as arche menelas to cover the Artificers for to mack Briges and there we law two Days the 12th we wend Back agin to flying arme which lay on the hill north of the fish Kill and there we lay until the 17th and that Day we layt town our arms by Capitulation.*

Obliged by the terms of surrender to return to Canada, many of the British, and the Americans who fought with them, embarked on their long journey north, some by land and others by water. Simmons undertook his trip with twenty-eight of his men:

> *And in the Convenon It was agreet the Volunteer Saillors artyficirs batone men must go to Canada and so we Croset the Rever that Day and wend as far as Bathen Kill and the 18th to fort Johnson and the 20th to for Gorge.*

103

Simmons was among the soldiers present as the British surrendered their arms to the Americans after the Battle of Saratoga. He was fortunate not to be held as a captive until the end of the war as was the case with many of his fellow men at arms. Print, 1800s.

From the Batten Kill to Fort George is twenty-seven miles. According to Simmons's journal, the trip took three days. They continued their journey with the sloop *Demon III* and a "butiacker" (thought by Dr. Burleigh to be a type of boat), heading farther up the lake, and eventually traveled by foot to Fort Ticonderoga. Simmons wrote: "We Came on *Dimon III* and took a Butiacker and Came that Day to the nine Mile Iland…and the 25th to Diante rogo."

The journal's transcriber, Dr. Burleigh, described the journey as "a most dispiriting time…and a most distressing situation." Simmons and his men were traveling by bateau in the last week of October in the face of a north wind blowing snow and rain. A typical bateau would have comfortably transported a crew and onboard party of twenty at the time, but by necessity Simmons was transporting almost a third more. Forced by weather and changing winds to come ashore on more than one occasion, they eventually arrived at Split Rock, about three miles north of Tichonderoga:

Lieutenant Henry Simmons

Simmons and his men reached Fort Ticonderoga on Lake Champlain after traveling by boat and by foot through inclement conditions of blowing snow and rain. *Sketch by the author.*

> *There we gat a batone and wend that Day a boud 8 mile the Wind in the North and there we lay still in the woods and a Storm from the north With Snow and a little Rain…and there we came about noon the wind Stle in the north it Rainth that afternoon and the next night the next Day the Wind came to the south and wend from thence the 29th as fare as Split Rock and there we lay wind bound.*

Simmons and his men reached Point Au Fer, New York, at the northern end of Lake Champlain a little more than a week after having left Ticonderoga by boat. They entered the Richelieu River, which drains Lake Champlain and the St. Lawrence, and eventually arrived at Fort St. Johns. They found no shelter at the former French fort and were forced to sleep in the woods during their first night in Canada. They were left with no choice but to continue traveling and headed west along the south shore of the St. Lawrence to Longeuil, across the river from the Island of Montreal:

Lachine, Quebec, was a tranquil village when Simmons arrived with his men on December 9, 1777. A century earlier, the community had been destroyed in a retributive raid by a Mohawk war party. Print, 1800s.

From thence five mile to the north of point to faire…the 3th about noon we arift as Saint Johns and there we lay that night in the woods and we wend about nine miles there we layet with Some french men…then the 6th we wend to Lang gale.

After experiencing some difficulty crossing the river, they managed to reach the far shore and found lodging for several nights on the island: "The west Supbub of Montreal the 8th we wend up to Lachenne there we stayt that night the 9th we was billetet in the St. Suse."

At this point, Simmons and his men had been gone from Claverack for almost four months and from Saratoga for three weeks, and they found themselves in a foreign land almost 400 miles north of their homes. The remainder of Simmons's career was marred by an unpleasant event in 1779 in which he received "a decent cudgelling" at the hands of Major James Rogers, according to a citation noted by historian J.J. Talman. To pursue their Loyalist grants, they were obligated to travel east to Quebec City, a journey of another 180 miles. They completed that trip in two weeks. There, Simmons's journal fell silent.

Of the twenty-eight men who made the trek, one-third were teenagers, ten were in their twenties, four were in their thirties and Simmons himself was thirty-seven years of age. In December 1783, the Loyalist corps were reduced and the lands along the St. Lawrence and Cataraqui Rivers were ordered surveyed.

It took the men several years to receive their grants and to be reunited with their families. In 1784, Lieutenant Simmons led more than four hundred men, women and children to settle in Ernestown County on the St. Lawrence River, past Kingston, more than 150 miles west of Montreal. Of the twenty-eight men who made the original trip from Claverack, and later Saratoga, eleven chose to settle in the area. The men were granted land according to their ranks, and land administrators made efforts to provide each of their families with food, clothing, arms, tools and seed.

Simmons took thirteen hundred acres of land slightly north of the St. Lawrence and began improvements that included an inn and saw-, flour and feed mills. He harnessed the "Big Creek" and gave the nearby road its name, Simmons Mills. The community became known as Wilton—Henry Simmons's middle name—and his mills continued in operation by Austin Simmons, his grandson, until the end of the nineteenth century.

As for his original hometown on the Hudson River in New York, Claverack was incorporated into the rapidly growing port city of Hudson that came within one vote of becoming the state capital. By 1790, Hudson was the eighth largest city in the United States.

Simmons's commanding officer, Captain Christian Wehr, settled in the village of Philipsburg, Quebec, near the Vermont border, where he died in 1824 at the age of ninety-two. Colonel Edward Jessup was awarded a land claim east of Kingston. He founded the town of Prescott, Ontario, where he "died of a palsy" in 1816 at the age of eighty.

The year of death and final resting place of Lieutenant Henry Simmons are unknown. There is conjecture that he is buried along the Big Creek in an unspecified location in the backyard of a sixth-generation descendant.

Chapter 8

MARY (MOLLY) BRANT

Descended from eminent Mohawks, Molly Brant encouraged her people to join the British side in the War of Independence. The Americans prevailed, and the heroine founder of Ontario passed her final days, diminished by her people though admired by whites, living in Kingston at the junction of the Rideau and St. Lawrence Rivers.

Few eighteenth-century North Americans were more colorful than Sir William Johnson, the British officer, estate owner and Indian administrator whose honest dealings with the Mohawks and mastery of their language endeared him to the native tribes. His victory over the French and Algonquians in 1755 at the Battle of Lake George, New York, earned him a British baronetcy. For a white man to be respected by both entities was no mean diplomatic feat in the middle and latter half of the 1700s.

Born in Ireland, Johnson arrived in New York in 1738 as a plucky young lawyer of lesser gentry. The enlightened twenty-three-year-old found a colony dominated by high-placed New Yorkers and British administrators in the southern reaches of the colony, so he headed north and west, where he became enamored with the stoic Iroquois. His naval hero and entrepreneurial uncle, Admiral Peter Warren of the British Royal Navy, had sent him to manage landholdings in the Mohawk Valley. Johnson quickly showed that he had a mind for business and leveraged the commission into a vast personal fortune.

Some called him the greatest frontiersman of the day. The Mohawk called him *Warraghiyagey*, a "man of many interests," in tribute to his irrepressible curiosity. William Johnson was passionate about commerce, literature, science, native culture and—as was not uncommon among his contemporaries—native women. His dalliances with aboriginal ladies

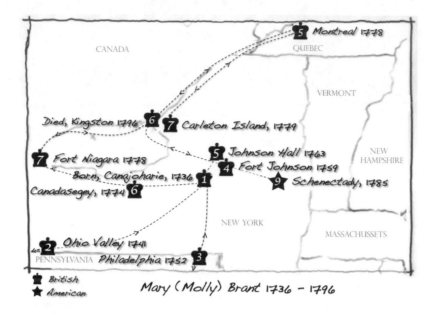

Molly Brant was born in Canajoharie on the Mohawk River (1), moved to the Ohio Valley as a child and later returned to the Mohawk Valley. She moved into Johnson Hall in her early twenties and died in 1796 in Kingston (11) on the St. Lawrence River. *Map by the author.*

throughout the New York colony were prodigious; he was rumored to have fathered hundreds of children. He was nonetheless highly regarded, and in 1751, when landholdings of 600,000 acres made him one of the richest men in the colonies, he picked fifteen-year-old Molly (Mary) Brant to join him at his side.

Those familiar with Molly's strong lineage, as Johnson was, might have predicted that she would grow into a native stateswoman of historic scope. She was born in 1736 in Canajoharie on the Mohawk River Valley and moved with her parents to the Ohio River as a young child. Its valley was a highly competitive frontier out of which Sioux and Shawnee natives were forced by Iroquois war parties. Land was not the objective of the interlopers—they wanted fur-skinned animals to sell to the Europeans, having already emptied their one-hundred-mile-long Mohawk Valley of such beasts.

Of the whites, the British were in the Ohio Valley for military reasons, and the Americans were moving west as speculators and colonizers. The French trappers were the most successful with the Iroquois, having learned to understand and respect native customs in order to curry favor.

Mary (Molly) Brant

Lands to the west of the "Great Falls of the Mohawk" are generally considered to be homelands for the Mohawks, the founding people of the Iroquois Confederacy. Print, 1700s.

Molly Brant was brought into this quilted turf by Peter, *Tehowaghwengaraghkwin*, and Margaret, *Owandah*. Historians generally agree that Margaret was a well-regarded clan mother in the matrilineal tradition of the Iroquois. However, historical accounts vary regarding her paternal line. For example, Peter Hendrick, *Theyanoguin*, the legendary Mohawk chief who died in 1755 at the Battle of Lake George, New York, is most often indicated as her father. By coincidence, another Mohawk chief of the Wolf Clan carried the same name. Peter Hendrick was one of the "Four Iroquois Kings" who visited Queen Anne in England in 1710. Suggestions that he may have been her father are sometimes discounted, as Molly was born twenty-six years after his trip to England. Alternative research suggests that Brant may have descended from yet another chief present at the court of Queen Anne, *Sagayeathquapiethtow* of the Bear Clan.

Whatever Molly's paternity, her father would have been a warrior of note who died not long after her young brother Joseph was born in 1741. After her husband's death, Margaret returned to her ancestral home along the Mohawk River and remarried a white man by the name of Brant. Molly and Joseph assumed his surname as descendants of intermarriages between whites and aboriginals customarily adopted the paternal family name as a courtesy.

Molly was trained by her mother in the tradition of sowing, cultivating and harvesting the "Three Sisters" of the Iroquois: corn, beans and squash. Molly

The Seven Years' War engulfed Europe and eventually reached North America as the French and Indian War. Major General William Johnson, Molly Brant's future husband in native ceremony, distinguished himself in battle at Lake George. Print, 1700s.

showed an uncommon intellect and an uncanny ability to mix medicinal plants and herbs, a skill that later saved many soldiers and natives, including the first governor of Upper Canada, John Graves Simcoe. Her diplomatic skills became apparent at an early age; as a teenager, she was included in a native entourage that paid a formal visit to Philadelphia for consultations with the governor of Pennsylvania.

Molly was described by a contemporary observer as "pretty, likely not having the small pox," clever and spirited. At the age of sixteen, she surprised a mustering regiment by jumping on the back of a young officer's startled horse and taking them both on a wild ride, to the amusement and amazement of the crowd. The officer was a colonel at the time and the man for whom she had affection: William Johnson.

Molly's carefree days were cut short by the French and Indian War. In 1755, the British and Mohawks, led by Johnson and King Hendrick respectively, moved south and east with the intention of driving the French out of the Lake George and Lake Champlain corridors. Johnson was in his prime as a commander but was considered no match for the French Hessian commander, Baron de Dieskau.

Johnson sent a young officer and an old chief, Colonel Ephraim Williams and King Hendrick, to scout the French as they advanced toward Lake George. Dieskau had intelligence that a British and Mohawk party was traveling the narrow road to Fort Edward and was susceptible to ambush. The baron arranged his men in the shape of a hook and closed in just as Williams sensed the trap.

After his horse was shot out from under him, Williams climbed atop a rock and shouted to rally his troops. Molly's grandfather, King Hendrick, was shot and killed; moments later, Williams took a bullet to the head for his bravery. French and native guns mowed down the surrounded British and Mohawks in the skirmish, later named the "Bloody Sunday Scout."

Unbowed by the deaths, Johnson barricaded his men behind stumps and wagons and faced down the German aristocrat as his French troops advanced. The upper hand passed back and forth throughout the day. Johnson was shot in the leg and fought on; the baron, overconfident from the earlier engagement, was shot three times.

Sir William Johnson's gentlemanly reputation may have led the badly wounded Dieskau to order his men to leave him behind and retreat just as the British militia breached the French barricades. As dusk settled on the Battle of Lake George, the French had suffered three times the casualties of the British, and Johnson emerged victorious. Dieskau was taken to Fort Edward, where he was placed on a cot in Johnson's tent; later, he was brought to Johnson's home for an extended convalescence and ultimately returned to France, where he died from his wounds.

For his role in the fray, Molly's uncle Nickus was subsequently imprisoned by the French in Quebec along with other Six Nations warriors who were soon ransomed back by Johnson, who was made a baronet as a result of his heroics at Fort George. While Nickus was incarcerated, Johnson cared for the Brant family, and it was during this time that his and Molly's fondness for each other deepened.

In 1759, at the age of twenty-three, Molly moved into Johnson's stone mansion, Johnson Hall, became his chatelaine and adopted several of his children born out of wedlock. Their marriage was Mohawk and was not accompanied by an Anglican ceremony, as Johnson was already legally married at the time. Molly immediately took control of the household, managing its many slaves, servants and staff, including Johnson's secretary and bookkeeper. Native chiefs, sachems, judges, governors, lords and ladies all luxuriated in Molly's hospitality at Johnson Hall, while she advocated for Mohawk interests in the many treaty discussions that took place there. One such conference involved more than ninety Indians staying in her house while Molly acted as translator, negotiator and hostess to the proceedings.

Her duty list grew during Johnson's many absences and illnesses, which resulted from his war injuries. She oversaw crop harvesting, food inspection

Johnson received his baronet status, the first granted in North America, for his victory at the Battle of Lake George in 1755. He and Molly Brant were among the most influential men and women in North American Indian affairs in the eighteenth century. *Courtesy of Kelly Hunter.*

114

and the complaints of tenant farmers. In 1773, she helped six hundred Scottish Highlanders, destitute since the Battle of Culloden, settle near her estate at the invitation of her husband.

Molly flourished in both Mohawk and colonial British society, often mixing the wardrobes of both with great flair. Respect flowed naturally from her matrilineal people, and she leveraged it to become a leader on her own terms. The British were often in awe of her powers of persuasion. William Claus, an associate of Johnson's, once said, "One word from her is more taken notice of by the five Nations than a thousand from any white Man without Exception."

Johnson died of a stroke in 1774, leaving inheritances for Molly and his known children; his estate passed to his son John. Molly and her children returned to her ancestral home at Canajoharie, where, along with her brother, she operated a store to trade among the Indians. The War of Independence had forced Loyalists to flee to the forests, and Molly responded by supplying food and ammunition to those in hiding.

Farther east, Patriot rebels forced their way into the Mohawk Valley and began to intimidate and strong-arm Loyalists. Midway in the valley Sir John

Mary Brant ran the household at Johnson Hall in addition to providing leadership to the Iroquois Confederacy. Not all of the native sachems agreed with her support of the British. *Courtesy of Kelly Hunter.*

Johnson strengthened the defense of Johnson Hall in anticipation of an assault. His small militia was no match for the three thousand men sent by General Philip Schuyler to disarm him. Schuyler, once a friend of Sir William and Molly, initially accepted John Johnson's offer to remain neutral. However, Molly later learned that Schuyler was intent on betraying John and had sent an advance party to arrest him. She managed to send a warning just in time, and John escaped to Montreal, leading his tenant farmer families on an arduous, exhausting flight to safety. The rebels stormed Johnson Hall with fury, desecrating Sir William's grave, melting down his leaden casket for bullets and scattering and plundering his remains.

In September 1777, Molly and her brood were forced to flee from Canajoharie to Canadasegey, near present-day Geneva, New York. She was in danger of being hanged as a spy, since her brother Joseph's victory a month earlier at the bloody Battle of Oriskany had been aided by her dispatches on British troop movements. Already threatened by local rebels and their Committee of Safety, she survived at least two late-night raids on her house. Once the Americans learned of her secret service, they encouraged the turncoat Oneidas to burn and sack her home, which they did, taking much of the money, gold and silver jewelry and fine clothing that Molly had left behind.

Molly and her brother Joseph vowed to avenge their losses. The next year, Joseph tore into the upper Susquehanna Valley, burned towns and forts and led what became known as the Cherry Valley Massacre. His name struck fear among the rebels, and he secured his reputation as an indomitable opponent. As Joseph turned from diplomat to combatant, Molly took up residence as negotiator at Fort Niagara, a British fort that her husband had won from the French two decades earlier.

She served as the channel between the British forces and the Iroquois until she heard that her two sons, Peter and William, had been killed in action. Bitter and vengeful, she sought the head of an American officer who had led attacks against Joseph's forces and had been jailed at Niagara. He was able to escape Molly's wrath because his commanding officer sent him to Montreal, "for fear of what the Indians might do to him." Interestingly, Molly was later called to Montreal, but no harm came to the officer while she was there.

In Montreal, Molly pined for her mother and children back in Niagara. Widowed, lonely and with her grown sons dead, she headed up the St. Lawrence River to Carleton Island, where Governor Haldimand asked her to be a political instrument, used for "encouraging the Indians to preserve their fidelity." The island, located across from present-day Alexandria Bay on the New York side, was selected as the post from which Britain would defend

Mary (Molly) Brant

Molly Brant managed to maintain order among Iroquois warriors temporarily placed at Fort Haldimand on Carleton Island in the St. Lawrence River after the war. St. Regis became the nearest reserve to the east and Tyendinaga to the west. Print, 1800s.

Molly Brant helped the first lieutenant governor of Upper Canada, John Graves Simcoe, recover from a serious illness in 1795, the year before she died. The specific location of her final resting place in a Kingston churchyard is not known. Print, 1800s.

the river from Montreal to the Great Lakes. Its housing conditions were deplorable, and the wintering Indians grumbled, though Molly managed to keep them in good behavior and sober.

When the Six Nations confederacy was overlooked in the peace treaty of 1783, it was apparent that Molly's decade of loyalty to the Crown had not been taken into account or in the very least, had not been rewarded. She had run out of inheritance and was shunned by the other native leaders.

Later that year, Governor Haldimand ordered a house to be built for Molly at the mouth of the Rideau on the Cataraqui River. She ventured back once to the Mohawk Valley in 1785, rejecting "with the utmost contempt" compensation from the Americans who tried to woo her to stay. In Cataraqui, present-day Kingston, she remained a devout Anglican until she died in 1796. The exact location of her grave at the St. Paul's cemetery is unknown.

Twentieth-century Canadian archaeologists unearthed the foundations of Molly's stone house in Kingston, two hundred years after Molly laid the foundations for Ontario.

Chapter 9

COLONEL JOEL STONE

Colonel Joel Stone was a Loyalist combatant operating out of New York and Long Island during the Revolutionary War. His personal fortunes continually rose and fell throughout his lifetime. His legacy became the town of Gananoque on the north shore of the St. Lawrence River, alongside the Thousand Islands.

In the early morning of September 12, 1812, Captain Benjamin Forsyth left Cape Vincent, New York, crossed the St. Lawrence River and attacked the small Upper Canada settlement of Gananoque. His well-armed U.S. Rifle Regiment outnumbered the town's defenders, the Leeds and Grenville militias, who managed to fire only a single round at the advancing Americans before falling back.

By the time the raid ended, the town had been drained of food and supplies, its depot burned and the home of the militia's affluent commander, Colonel Joel Stone, ransacked. Worse still, Stone's wife—his second—took a musket ball in her hip that was to maim her for life.

The War of 1812 was a stinging reminder to Stone of the forces that dogged him throughout his life. He had lost access to his Connecticut fortune and family decades earlier during the War of Independence. As a Loyalist, he was captured, imprisoned and stripped of his possessions; as a businessman, he pursued riches as a merchant, privateer and mill owner. Eventually he fled to England, and later Canada, in search of entrepreneurial opportunity. He founded Gananoque, on the north shore of the St. Lawrence River, where he lived in exile from his homeland for the remainder of his turbulent life.

Stone was born in 1740 into a middle-class family on the north shore of Long Island Sound in the town of Guilford, Connecticut. His antecedents had arrived from England a century earlier and settled in the nearby

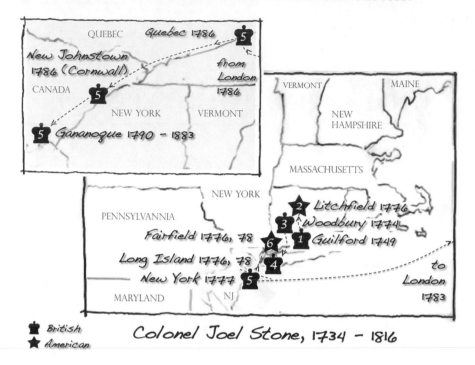

Colonel Joel Stone was an American entrepreneur who saw much action in the Long Island region of New York (4, 5) during the Revolutionary War. Afterward, he founded the Canadian community of Gananoque (5), the "Gateway to the Thousand Islands." *Map by the author.*

Algonquian territory of Quinnipiac, the "land of the sleeping giant." He was the second son of Stephen Stone, a farmer who eventually married twice and fathered a total of sixteen children. The family moved north to Litchfield, Connecticut, where they owned and operated a farm. Here, Joel Stone's entrepreneurial instincts first emerged.

Stone set out to improve the family's fortune after a succession of deaths left him, as the eldest surviving son, with the responsibility for the well-being of the entire family. Farming was difficult in the rough terrain of western Connecticut, and merchants were more likely to prosper financially and politically. In 1771, Stone became the quintessential traveling salesman, moving about the countryside selling items to farmers.

By 1774, Stone began operating out of Woodbury, a larger, more commercially viable town to the south. According to Timothy Compeau, Stone's recent biographer, Stone entered into partnership with the most successful businessman in the area with assets of $1 million, a monumental sum for eighteenth-century New England. Together, they traded with

Colonel Joel Stone

Joel Stone's Connecticut house still stands. Built in 1774, it demonstrated Stone to be a man of means at a relatively young age. The house provided lodgings for him and for other members of his birth family. *Sketch by the author.*

merchants in the nearby emerging megalopolis of New York City and with British and foreign holdings in the Caribbean.

Stone's affluent life was threatened with the first rumblings of revolution, though his interests lay more in profits than in politics. By mid-decade, he had built a substantial home to house himself and his unmarried sisters. His father became increasingly vocal in his disdain for American independence, while Joel prudently avoided taking a position publicly.

It was Stone's misfortune to live in Connecticut. Hostilities broke out in the Boston area and advanced south along the Atlantic seaboard toward New York. The Sons of Liberty, which had been a secret organization, went public with calls for resistance against Crown taxes and laws. Its splinter groups were scattered throughout the thirteen colonies, including Connecticut, and their demonstrations inevitably turned into violent mobs. When the Liberty Sons formed in a town square, Loyalists inevitably found themselves in great peril as Patriots, angered with the British colonial administration, made them targets.

In southern Connecticut, the British navy bombarded the coastal roads along Long Island Sound and made movement of troops and supplies extremely dangerous for the rebel army. To General George Washington, bombardments meant that a northern supply route was a matter of urgency, and he chose Litchfield because it offered a defensible location for a depot.

Perched on a high plateau protected by a palisade and guardhouse, it was "the least exposed to the incursions of the English," according to Washington. The Yankees of upper Connecticut paid a high price for the security of a heavy military presence. The demand for comestibles for Washington's Continental army drove prices up, and many merchants, Joel Stone and his partners included, fell into disfavor for suspicion of trading with the enemy.

Stone's affairs were complicated further by religion: he was Anglican at a time when the Church of England was perceived to be an extension of Britain's imperious rule. According to Compeau, Stone wrote in 1775 that while his business volumes increased daily, he "would sooner perish in the general calamity than abet in the least degree the enemies of the British constitution."

In addition to its fortress-like supply depot, Litchfield became notorious for aggressive rebel gangs, Continental army garrisons and its prison, one of the most wretched in the colonies. Notable prisoners were housed there, including William Franklin, the Loyalist and illegitimate son of Benjamin Franklin, and Ensign Roger Stevens, a frontier spy captured from the British army's Northern Department. Stevens survived the war and eventually became the first settler on the northern length of the Rideau River.

Stone heard public outcries slandering his business partners and family that served to stoke his anger toward the Patriots. After the arrest of his father, he decided to actively denounce the republican cause and adopt a militant stance. Rebels soon uncovered that Stone had conspired to free the imprisoned mayor of New York, who had been charged with plotting the assassination of George Washington, and a mob gathered to arrest him. He fled and was tracked for days by vigilantes, but he managed to escape by boat across to Long Island.

The British leadership, forced to evacuate Boston, gathered troops in Nova Scotia and sailed south from Halifax to Long Island Sound. The deposed governor of New Hampshire, Sir John Wentworth, formed a Loyalist brigade in New York into which Stone enlisted.

Meanwhile, during Stone's absence from Connecticut, his house was ransacked and his property appropriated by the rebel commission. With

General Washington took command of the Continental army in New York City in
the summer of 1776. By mid-November, Manhattan was in the hands of the British.
Washington, though, returned victorious during the British evacuation in 1783. Print, 1800s.

money scarce and living far-removed from his family, Stone resorted to the unsavory practice of recruitment and signed up with the wealthy New Yorker Brigadier General Oliver DeLancey, helping to raise several brigades. Of the three formed, two went to Florida and engaged in the southern campaign with some success; the third remained in New York and was instrumental in maintaining the city as a British stronghold.

DeLancey's men served as guards and police officers in the city and protectors of Fort Franklin on Long Island. Armed rebel parties often crossed from the Connecticut shore, and during a raid in early 1778, they captured Stone and brought him back from imprisonment in Fairfield. He later wrote of his time in jail, "[I had] to suffer every Rigor that Rebel Malice could suggest, in close Confinement for a Considerable period of time." Fortunately for Stone, Fairfield was far less secure than Litchfield, and he was able to escape in May of that year.

Stone headed to the safety of New York City and turned to privateering to earn his living, though during his first outing he almost lost his life in a shipwreck. His second tour was onboard the brigantine *Halifax*, aboard which, according to one of his shipmates, he "landed in the face of continual fire from the Rebels; then took Command of a party of Marines where he was much exposed and during the whole Expedition exerted himself in a very Spirited manner."

Stone also saw action on land in the service of New York governor Thomas Tyron in an extended raid against the towns of New Haven and Fairfield, the latter being the same town in which he had been imprisoned the year earlier. Stone's future brightened in 1799 when, as captain in the New York City militia, he married Leah Moore, the daughter of a prosperous mariner who provided the couple with a house and a dowry. But his birth family was in disarray back in Connecticut, with his younger brother working for the Litchfield rebel militia and the rest suffering through bouts of smallpox. His sister Dothe took on the burden of caring for their aging father while feeding the family.

Stone's marriage was a success financially but less so romantically. His wife had been raised in a comfortable household, and "the men in her life portrayed her as demanding and temperamental," according to historian Janice Potter-MacKinnon. Her eccentric father was continually at sea, much to the emotional detriment of his daughter. When her mother died in 1782, her father returned in grief and quickly met a nineteen-year-old woman, whom he married within a month.

Leah Moore's state of mind around this time was poor. Her husband experienced a bout with a mysterious illness during which his business failed.

The unknown malady plagued him continually through his life and on several occasions impeded his ability to generate income. On this occasion, Stone's financial stress was compounded with the birth his son, Stephen Jr.

With the end of the war upon the signing of the Treaty of Paris in 1783, Stone's life remained in turmoil. He returned to Connecticut but found that he was unwelcome owing to a law that banished Loyalists with the threat of a lashing upon their return. He was pointedly given two days to leave the colony and did so when he discovered that other laws had been enacted that effectively branded him as treasonous and placed a price on his head.

Much to Leah's disappointment, Stone did not stay in New York but instead sailed to England in search of compensation from the British for the loss of his possessions and properties in Connecticut. In his petition to the Crown, he claimed he had been "deprived...of Property to the Amount of Fifteen Hundred Pounds Sterling, and reduced...to real want, with a wife and Children to support on Thirty Pounds per Annum, granted to him by the Treasury as an American sufferer."

In London in 1783, he met Sir Guy Carleton and became familiar with the plans for Loyalist grants on the north shore of the St. Lawrence River; meanwhile, his estranged wife, Leah, refused to reply to any of his correspondence. According to Potter-MacKinnon, Stone's letters were supportive and affectionate and often contained money to assist Leah

Joel Stone returned from London and came ashore at Quebec in 1786. He and the eminent Sir John Johnson had a dispute over the lands Stone had claimed on the north shore of the St. Lawrence River. The Quebec Lands Office ruled in Stone's favor. Print, 1800s.

Stone's marriage to New Yorker Leah Moore fell into a ruined state shortly after he returned from England. He sent her from Canada back to New York and moved his children to Hartford, Connecticut, to be schooled. Print, 1800s.

with the family. But her father wrote to Stone in England, stating, "Her behavior is so most unaccountable that it is not in my power to doing anything for her."

Stone stayed in London for three more years while navigating the colonial bureaucracy in search of compensation for his losses and to free up an inheritance due his wife from a deceased uncle. He returned to North America in 1786, having been unsuccessful in negotiating either. Stone arrived at Quebec and moved upriver along the St. Lawrence, settling at New Johnstown, near the site of present-day Cornwall. According to historian Donald Harman Atkinson, Stone wrote in 1787, "I find it as good land in general as I ever set my foot on." Unfortunately, most of the good land had been claimed by Loyalists prior to his arrival, and Stone had to rely on his entrepreneurial instincts once more. He built a brew house for three stills and set up shop as a distiller.

His happy return to North America quickly soured, as he was underfunded and his debts mounted. His truculent wife left New York and came north to join him in Canada, where she gave birth to their second child, Mary. But the marital discord continued; Leah abhorred life in the wilderness. Stone sent her back to New York and petitioned for a legal separation that awarded a hefty maintenance agreement to Leah. So bitter was he that he advertised "to forbid anyone to credit my wife, Leah Stone, on my account as I will not pay any debts she may contract," according to a modern edition of the *Cataraqui Town Crier*. He had Stephen and Mary removed from Leah's home and placed them in school in Hartford, Connecticut.

Stone scouted for land on which he could base a larger business and selected the lands farther west along the St. Lawrence on both sides of the mouth of the Gananoque River. The property's location was ideal to generate water power for a mill site. His agent submitted a request to the land board for five hundred acres on each side of the river, but a dispute ensued with his good friend and Loyalist leader Sir John Johnson, who also submitted a claim for the same land. Eventually, the Quebec Land Office conceded that Stone's claim had preceded Johnson's, and he was able to start business anew, building a sawmill and a gristmill.

Stone prospered yet again, and in so doing, he founded the town of Gananoque, where he lived an affluent and initially solitary life. In 1791, Leah Moore Stone died in New York, and in 1799 Stone married Abigail Dayton, a widow from the shores of Lake Huron. Ten years later, his daughter returned from the United States to marry the son of his business partner, Charles McDonald. His own son, William, also returned to act as Stone's heir, but after a few successful years, he took ill and died.

Stone's businesses continued to expand as he acquired titles and official offices, including roads commissioner, customs collector, colonel of the militia and justice of the peace. But international peace ended in 1812 with the declaration of war against Britain by the United States under the leadership of President James Madison. Stone continued to trade with the American side right up to the time when Captain Forsyth launched his attack on Gananoque that September.

The target of Forsythe's Riflemen Regiment was not only Gananoque's supply depot but also the town's founder, Stone, who was still widely considered a traitor almost thirty years after leaving the breakaway colonies. The American invaders burned the depot, fired on Stone's house and wounded his wife. Stone, who was not present at the time, returned to discover the chaotic scene. His wife eventually recovered, but with a limp, and Stone charged several militiamen with fleeing the scene of the skirmish.

At the end of hostilities in 1814, Stone's turbulent life settled into one of comfortable living. Two decades later, he died peacefully in 1833 at the age of eighty-four, having outlived both of his wives, most of his family and many of those who had banished him from his homeland.

In the eighteenth century, Colonel Joel Stone was a frustrated family man, a stalwart solider and an irrepressible entrepreneur in the American tradition.

Thanks to Stone's mills, Gananoque began as an industrial site at the end of the eighteenth century and evolved into a recreational launch point for the Thousand Islands in modern times. Print, 1800s.

Colonel Joel Stone

In the twenty-first century, his complexities have been aptly described by historian Timothy Compeau, who writes of Stone:

> *His diligent pursuit of money, the hint of self-importance and his early marital discord...troubling...he was neither a villain nor a saint...an exceptional man, but also a flawed human being, [whose] perseverance in the face of loss and hardship is admirable.*

Chapter 10

DR. GEORGE SMYTH

British "master spy" Dr. George Smyth gathered intelligence as he worked under watchful rebel eyes in a military hospital in Albany. Enlisting the help of his wife, sons and brother, the crafty Smyth made spying a family affair. His name, slightly altered, eventually lent itself to the town of Smiths Falls on the Rideau Canal.

The seventeenth-century poem "Hudibras" was a satirical tale of a faux hero who was a bumbling rebel. Intending to mock Oliver Cromwell and the Roundheads who murdered King Charles I of England, its cagey and witty author, Samuel Butler, wisely chose to publish the comedy only after the monarchy was restored and Cromwell was dead, his body exhumed, hanged and beheaded.

Equally wry was the erudite spy Dr. George Smyth of Fort Edward, New York. Smyth left Ireland in 1770 to pursue a more challenging medical career in the colonies. By all accounts, he was a superb doctor whose skills were in great demand by the time war broke out in the second half of the decade.

Before long, Smyth was applying his intellect to more than tending injured Loyalists: he became a British frontier spy. Aptly, he chose "Hudibras" as his code name.

Governor Haldimand and the British northern army based in Quebec sought much-needed intelligence on the movements of the American regulars and rebels in the New York colony during the Revolutionary War. Smyth had come to him highly recommended as a spy by Sir John Johnson, son of the baronet who had been knighted for bravery at the Battle of Lake George, New York, in the Seven Years' War.

The fact that Smyth adopted the code name Hudibras suggested to Haldimand that his new charge was as literate and comical as he was clever.

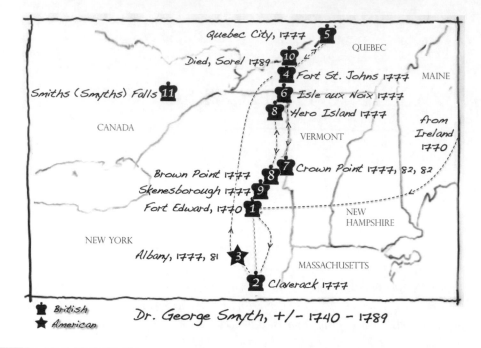

Quebec City, 1777 **5**
Died, Sorel 1789 **10**
QUEBEC
4 Fort St. Johns 1777 MAINE
Smiths (Smyths) Falls **11**
6 Isle aux Noix 1777
8 Hero Island 1777
from Ireland 1770
CANADA
VERMONT
7 Crown Point 1777, 82, 82
Brown Point 1777 **8**
Skenesborough 1777 **9**
Fort Edward, 1770 **1**
NEW HAMPSHIRE
NEW YORK
Albany, 1777, 81 **3**
MASSACHUSETTS
2 Claverack 1777

British
American

Dr. George Smyth, +/- 1740 - 1789

Dr. George Smyth became second in command of the British army's Northern Department Spy Corps. He died in Sorel, Quebec (10), shortly after the war, and his abridged name was lent to the town of Smiths Falls (11) on the Rideau Canal. *Map by the author.*

He was right; the doctor could not resist extending the joke to his son Terence, who became a spy under the code name "Young Hudibras."

Young Hudibras, his brother Thomas, his uncle Patrick, his father George and his mother, who only ever identified herself as "R.J.," became a family devoted to the secret service. Their cleverness helped them survive abductions, rebel jails and long periods in irons. Incredibly, they all survived the war and spent their final years living in safety in Upper Canada.

The hard life of frontier spying eventually took its toll on Dr. Smyth, and he died in Sorel at Fort William Henry in 1789. Sons Terence and Thomas settled in Elizabethtown, the site of modern-day Brockville on the St. Lawrence River.

The brothers laid claim to one of the Rideau River's top three mill sites: Terence built a mill on the Burritts Rapids site. The entrepreneurial William Merrick, a distant relative of the Smyths through marriage, built a mill on another top site seven miles upstream, ultimately lending his name to the community that sprang up around his mill.

Dr. George Smyth

Ever the opportunist, Merrick protected the Smyth name on the only remaining mill site to ensure that no competition could build there. Although Thomas Smyth lost control of his claim to that site in the 1820s, the name Smyth—like the chameleon family itself—survived several incarnations before and after the opening of the Rideau Canal in 1832. The site, which boasts three Rideau Canal locks, has been officially known as Smiths Fall since 1883.

Dr. George Smyth might have found humor in the misspelling of the family name. His reputation for mirth was well known; less well known was his use of it to mask his fierce love of spying and intrigue. Smyth was not to be taken lightly, as Ensign Roger Stevens discovered when Smyth brought charges against him for the mishandling of accounts. Nor did the rebels dispute his acumen as a master spy. They captured him on four occasions, only to see him rescued or escaped on all but one.

Smyth settled with his wife and sons by Fort Edward. He built a house in 1777 on property given to him by his successful brother Patrick, a lawyer who had arrived in the colonies twenty years earlier. Patrick acquired land in the vicinity of the fort from prominent New Yorkers such as Philip Schuyler, the Yankee judge who became a member of the Continental Congress, a general in the Continental army and a target of abduction by Dr. Smyth during wartime.

Patrick did his own share of spying and, like his brother George, barely concealed his dislike of republican ideals. According to historian Hazel Mathews, Dr. Smyth was among the first to stand against the Patriots; upon the outbreak of hostilities, he immediately headed to Albany to set up a network of spies to carry dispatches to British commanders.

In July 1777, General "Gentleman Johnny" Borgoyne used Patrick's house as his British headquarters. Only a year before, the rebel Schuyler had used Patrick's nearby tavern as a courthouse. While Patrick's house was bustling with military officers coming and going, George's home offered quiet respite to frightened Loyalist settlers. In March of the next year, both brothers were apprehended and jailed on suspicion of spying.

Released on orders to report before the local "Board of Commissioners for the Detection and Defeating of Conspiracies," the indignant Smyths continued their spying ways, were captured a second time and spent the next three months in a rebel jail. Upon their second release, the brothers operated risky intelligence operations despite constant surveillance by rebels.

The original British spy networks under Sir Guy Carleton were made up of army regulars, as colonials were thought to be better suited to serving as guides. They were familiar with the frontier trails that led north alongside New York's Hudson River through Lake Champlain and into the Richelieu

Patrick Smyth, brother of Dr. George Smyth, built his house in Fort Edward, New York, in 1772. Members of the Smyth family were known to engage in espionage, including Patrick, who was arrested in his home by Benedict Arnold in 1777. *Courtesy of Kelly Hunter.*

River in Quebec. Some soon found themselves in the more dangerous role of spy; others often meandered off their routes to visit friends and family—to the frustration of their commanding officers.

Since regulars wore uniforms, they were less likely to be tried and hanged as spies if captured. Frontiersmen dressed as civilians, on the other hand, could justifiably face the noose—and many did.

Upon replacing Carleton, Governor Frederick Haldimand asked the intrepid Loyalist Justus Sherwood to lead his spy corps. One of Sherwood's first assignments was to build a "Loyal Blockhouse" on North Hero Island, from which he would run spy networks into New York and beyond.

George Smyth's sons Terence and Thomas followed their father and uncle into the spy trade, and their mother was not far behind. Between prison stays, the surgeon Smyth was employed in a rebel military hospital and, unknown to the enemy, his spy network remained intact. Mrs. "R.J." Smyth acted as his replacement, taking his dispatches and often passing them along using her own sons as messengers.

Dr. Smyth vanished one day when he heard that charges were again coming his way. The unlucky Young Hudibras was captured and jailed in Albany, where he languished for months. At one point, his father was seized by rebels and seemed destined to join Terence in the Albany jail, but the

Dr. George Smyth

Spies were caught and hanged by both sides of the conflict. Of note was William Franklin, Benjamin Franklin's Loyalist son, who avoided the noose but spent two years in a Patriot prison. Print, 1800s.

senior Smyth managed to escape with the help of daring British spy Mathew Howard, an agent of Justus Sherwood. Howard likely spirited Smyth away while the rebel guards were sleeping, taking the aging doctor over rough terrain to Point Au Fer on Lake Champlain. From there, he traveled by boat to Fort St. Johns, arriving exhausted and in poor health.

Eventually, Dr. Smyth had an audience with Governor Haldimand in Quebec City. The governor sensed that the bespectacled doctor was cagey and smart, and although he was older and more experienced than Justus Sherwood, Haldimand selected him as deputy to the new spy chief. Together they were responsible for recruiting spies, capturing enemy intelligence officers and managing the sensitive matter of prisoner exchanges.

The fortifications on Isle de Noix on the Richelieu River just across the United States–Canada border originated in 1759. American troops controlled it briefly during the Revolutionary War. Print, 1800s.

An uneasy relationship existed between the two from the start. On one occasion, Smyth pretended that Sherwood was his deputy, though the opposite was true. Smyth did nothing to offset rumblings among the men that Sherwood had been a Yankee Green Mountain Boy in Vermont, crossing over to the British only after an altercation with Ethan and Ira Allen. The rumors, though based in fact, needlessly brought the loyalty of the senior officer into question. Sherwood ignored the obstreperous doctor and stood stoic in the face of a whisper campaign. Sherwood was universally respectful both of his superiors and of men under his command. Smyth, on the other hand, was theatrical and often deliberately upstaged the younger Sherwood.

George Smyth's health suffered permanently as a result of the arduous trek from the filthy jail in Albany to the more commodious Fort St. Johns. He continued to stay at the fort for health reasons, while Sherwood and his men roughed it out in the newly built island blockhouse. From Fort St. Johns, Smyth often disobeyed Sherwood's orders and sent agents directly into the field, despite his senior officer's concern that rebels scouting for a particular British agent might stumble across more of his men unintentionally.

Sherwood was likely in the right, but his complaints to Haldimand were rebuffed. According to historian Mary Beacock Fryer in *Kings Men*, the governor's secretary even urged Sherwood "to be less touchy."

Dr. George Smyth

Spies carried dispatches concealed in the shafts of feather pens and inside musket balls and bone-handled knives. Partially hollowed books were sometimes used to conceal small weapons. *Sketch by the author.*

Sherwood and Smyth forced themselves to find a professional balance in deference to the dangers faced by their men. As a result, their spy networks worked efficiently for several years. Originally, the spy corps had been run unevenly under Carleton, but as the British prepared to invade New York from Quebec, Haldimand needed a professional secret service to acquire timely and accurate reconnaissance, and Sherwood and Smyth were able to provide it.

Each spy under the command of Sherwood and Smyth was outfitted with a short rifle, a musket, pocket pistols, a powder horn and a bullet pouch. For hacking their way through the bush and hand-to-hand fighting, tomahawks hung from their belts at the ready.

Dispatches were typically destined for Governor Haldimand in Quebec or Governor Clinton in New York, and they described everything from the price of wheat and rum to the movements of the Continental army. Yankee newspapers were also much sought-after, and British agents frequently stitched them into their coats for concealment. Often deliberately sealed in lead, dispatches would be tossed into the bush during moments of danger for later recovery. Messages were given in tightly rolled paper to fit into a quill pen or to be swallowed in case of capture. George's brother Patrick was said to prefer to conceal his messages in the handle of his hunting knife.

Throughout the early stages of the spy corps, Young Hudibras often found himself jailed in Albany—more out of recklessness than ineptitude. His brother Thomas was a lieutenant in the King's Royal Regiment under Sir John Johnson and appears to have been more cautious, according to historian Glenn Lockwood, as he was never caught, despite numerous assignments in the secret service. "It was a feat neither his father nor brother could boast, and it suggests as well a man willing to take no chances in life." He may also have just been lucky. Once, while escorting prisoners of war to an exchange, he encountered his mother, who had fled Albany.

During one of Terence's lengthier imprisonments, the Smyths implored Clinton to do all that he could to set Young Hudibras free. Before Clinton could take action, however, Terence saw to it himself: he escaped and headed for Vermont. He received protection under Ethan and Ira Allen and was reunited with a British scouting party and soon returned to action. Rarely did the entire Smyth family remain free; the daring Terence would soon find himself behind bars once again.

In the final stages of the war, the British experienced an increasing number of defeats, as did Dr. Smyth in three major operations with Justus Sherwood. The first was a bold plan to abduct Smyth's Yankee nemesis, General Philip Schuyler; the second was to burn a ship under construction for the renowned privateer John Paul Jones; and the third was to meet secretly with the Allen brothers and negotiate the return of Vermont to the British colonies.

Events, in all cases, conspired against them.

Schuyler was on his estate in the Hudson Valley when he was told by a friendly Loyalist of the plan to kidnap him. He went on the alert with increased security and armed guards. Within days, Indian and British kidnappers surrounded his house, broke through his door, hurled a tomahawk that narrowly missed his wife and began to plunder his house. Schuyler avoided capture. His unarmed bodyguards (they were sleeping in the basement) were able to prevent the abduction but were overwhelmed and hauled off to prison in Canada. Terence Smyth was about to be paroled when the raid took place. During interrogation, he refused to disclose potential hiding places or routes taken by the aspiring kidnappers and was returned to jail.

The case of John Paul Jones frustrated Smyth too. The French, who sided with the rebel colonies, were financing the building of a sixty-two-gun ship for

One audacious but unsuccessful plan of the British spy corps was to destroy a French-financed gun ship under construction for Captain John Paul Jones in Portsmouth, New Hampshire. Print, 1800s.

Jones in Portsmouth Harbor, New Hampshire. The spymasters managed to plant two of their men as workers on the construction site with the intention of setting the ship ablaze. The overly cautious men were never able to do so despite Jones's mistaken thinking that his ship would be raided from the sea. By the time the workers had prepared their arson, the war had ended and the ship had been christened and sent overseas for service in Russia.

Finally, the Green Mountain Boys—the militiamen in Vermont—played the Americans and the British off one another in order to broker the best deal for their tiny republic. The British believed that bringing Vermont into the fold could drive a wedge between the remaining thirteen colonies.

Secret meetings staged by British agents such as Roger Stevens enabled Sherwood to meet with his former Vermont colleagues Ethan and Ira Allen. Sherwood, who liked the former and loathed the latter, wisely brought Smyth to present terms of negotiation. The Allen brothers remained coy to the point where Sherman and Smyth realized they were being played. Negotiations ended with the conclusion of the war; Vermont eventually became the fourteenth American state.

By this time, the two spies had settled their differences. The doctor had helped his superior survive a near deadly bout of smallpox in 1783 and tended to his wife, Sarah, and children while Sherwood was stricken. Sherwood had often times sent his men out to retrieve Smyth's son Terence from jail, as he came to respect the entire family, despite the father's capricious behavior.

The Smyth family moved to Canada when the spy network was ordered by Haldimand to disband. Sherwood, who had been a surveyor before the war, took up the assignment of laying out lots for Loyalists and their families on the north shore of the St. Lawrence River for hundreds of miles east and west of Montreal. Uncharacteristically, he lost his footing, fell from a raft and drowned in the river near Quebec City in 1798 at the age of fifty-one. His body was never found.

Where war had failed to separate the Smyth family, peacetime was successful. By then in ill health, Dr. Smyth moved permanently with his wife to the relative comfort of Fort William Henry in Sorel, Quebec. Their sons pursued their land claims along the St. Lawrence and north along the Rideau River in the same region as Roger Stevens had pioneered.

With the passing of George Smyth in 1789, his sons made additional claims for Rideau grants, including acreage lands owed to their deceased father. It all totaled several thousand acres and included their much sought-after mill site on the Rideau River east of Merrickville. According to Glenn Lockwood, Young Hudibras told a surveyor that he and his brother Thomas only made the claim to please their father in his final days and never expected to get the property.

Dr. George Smyth

Jones' Cut,
Smith Falls, Ont.

Ironically, Dr. George Smyth never set foot on his Loyalist grant on the Rideau Canal. The village that grew around it enjoyed prosperity during the steamboat and railroad eras. Postcard, 1800s.

Dr. George Smyth would have been disappointed to learn of the fate of their claim, as it was sold for taxes in 1830. He would have been pleased, however, to learn that it became the site of three Rideau Canal locks built by Colonel John By as part of Lord Wellington's plan to defend Canada against any future American invasion.

To his alter ego Hudibras, the lending of his misspelled family name to the surrounding town of Smiths Falls might have been humorous.

Chapter 11

SIR JOHN JOHNSON

Both Sir John Johnson and his father, William, were brave in battle and fiercely loyal to their king; in death, both suffered the ignominy of having their graves desecrated, one in Quebec and the other in New York.

The parallels were many and the differences few between the lives of Sir John Johnson and his father, Sir William Johnson. They were baronets with huge landholdings in their respective colonies, Upper Canada and New York; they were prodigious at fathering children; they held prestigious positions in the British colonial administration of native affairs; and they were both heroes who gamely fought in the name of their king.

Even in death, the two colonials eerily mirrored each other. Their funerals were grand affairs that native North American leaders chose to honor with their attendance. Later, the stately grave sites of both men were dishonored and desecrated, though each for different reasons.

At the height of the American Revolution in the eighteenth century, Sir William Johnson's grave at Johnson Hall, New York, was dug up by angry rebels who looted his coffin and scattered his remains. Sir John Johnson's Canadian grave was accidently bulldozed into a pit midway through the twentieth century (and may have been looted during the First World War).

In the time since, the former has been relocated to a nearby church in Johnstown, New York, and restoration of the latter in the Eastern Townships of Quebec is planned through the efforts of the United Empire Loyalists, professional archaeologists and interested historians on both sides of the border.

Of the two men, the father was born into less propitious circumstances than the son.

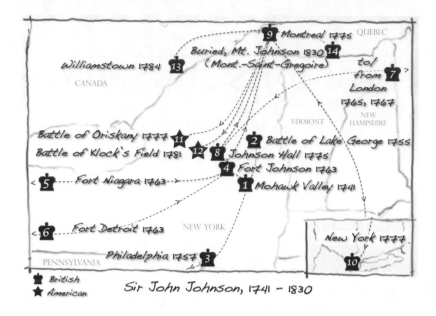

Sir John Johnson inherited his baronet title and his unwavering devotion to the Crown from his father. He made sure though that his family burial crypt on a mountain in the Eastern Townships of Quebec was built facing the United States. *Map by the author.*

William Johnson descended from an ancient line of Irishmen and was born at Smithtown, County Meath, Ireland, in 1715. His own father, Christopher, was three generations removed from Sir Turlough mac Henry Ó Néill, an Irish chieftain who tried, but failed, to straddle both sides of the Irish rebellion at the end of the sixteenth century and was forced to seek pardons for his family from Elizabeth I.

Christopher's father was named Thomas O'Neill MacShane. He incurred the wrath of Oliver Cromwell and felt obliged to adopt the name Johnson, the anglicized version of their old Irish family name of MacShane, which had, in turn, been related to the clan name of O'Neill.

An uncle of William Johnson's, Admiral Peter Warren, had risen to prominence in the British Royal Navy and acquired significant holdings in New York as a land speculator. Warren enjoyed fabulous wealth throughout his lifetime and continued to profit from successful marine campaigns in the Caribbean and the Atlantic, including the capture of the French fortress of Louisburg on Cape Breton Island in 1745.

Sir John Johnson

Warren enticed William to join him in the New World and, in 1738, hired him to manage his properties north and along the Mohawk River. At age twenty-three, William Johnson migrated north and west from New York City—then known as York City—to the Mohawk Valley and quickly proved to be an instinctive entrepreneur. He eventually built a fortune that surpassed his uncle's.

In so doing, William developed a fondness for Native Americans and their array of customs and cultures. He learned the art of native negotiation while buying their land from them and earned their respect by mastering their language. By age thirty-one, he was given considerable responsibility for Indian affairs, and three years later, in 1748, he was commissioned as a colonel and placed in command of fourteen companies of New York militiamen.

He emerged from the 1750s as a hero, having acquitted himself ably during the French and Indian Wars that consumed North America. William was wounded but emerged victorious from the Battle of Lake George, and the compassion that he showed to his defeated and injured counterpart, Baron Dieskau, earned him respect on both sides of the conflict. In a painting, the eminent American artist Benjamin West, who later painted the influential *The Death of General Wolfe*, depicted William's battlefield generosity to Dieskau, who eventually died from his wounds. William's victory, and his role in the seizures of Fort Niagara and Montreal after the French defeat at Quebec, earned him a British baronetcy.

As his fame, wealth and numerous responsibilities for Indian matters grew, so did his offspring. His sexual affairs bordered on wantonness: three children by Elizabeth Brant; another by her younger sister; eight by the legendary Molly Brant; three by Caroline Peters, who was the niece of the Mohawk chief King Hedrick; one by an Irishwoman Mary McGrath; and three by Catherine Weisenberg, a German immigrant and indentured servant. His intimacies extended to several other white and native women, but it was from his relationship with Weisenberg that John Johnson was born in November 1741.

John grew up in a bountiful household teeming with servants and slaves. His father's knighthood earned him thousands of acres in the Mohawk River Valley, and he built his first home, known as Mount Johnson, east of Amsterdam, New York, in 1743. Its location had long been known to natives as *Kalaneka* or "a place one stops to fill his bowl with food and drink"; its beautiful bluffs that sat atop a gentle creek flowing into the Mohawk made it a popular recreational haven for aboriginals. Many trails converged on the site, and it offered a natural location for the Johnsons to befriend Native Americans.

Sir John Johnson excelled in military matters, administration and land acquisition, particularly during his exile in Canada, where he oversaw the settling of thousands of displaced Loyalist New Yorkers. Portrait, 1800s.

At the age of thirteen, John Johnson joined his father at the Battle of Lake George, and two years later, in 1757, he began his formal education at the College and Academy of Philadelphia. His studies were intermittent, as the next year he was present at the capture of forts at Detroit and Niagara and at the important Indian councils held by his father in the field and back at Fort Johnson.

Just to the west of their first home, the Johnsons designed and built a Georgian stone house in 1759 called Fort Johnson—it had several outbuildings doubling as fortifications. The following year, at eighteen years of age, John's military career took hold, and he became a captain in the Tyron County militia.

Soon afterward, his father built yet another mansion farther inland on twenty thousand acres and named it Johnson Hall. This permitted John, in 1763, to take possession of Fort Johnson, where he lived for the next eleven years, a period that saw the family's businesses diversify beyond their milling and lumbering for German Palatine immigrants whom Sir William had sponsored to their New York colony. A town grew around Johnson Hall and attracted tradesmen associated with the needs of a frontier community, including a sword maker, a hatter, a breeches maker, an indentured shoemaker, a tanner, a wheelwright, a collar maker, a surveyor and a gunsmith.

With the plantation flourishing, William prevailed upon John to marry into the New York gentry, and in 1763 he wed Mary "Polly" Watts, the daughter of a prominent member of the Council of New York, a governing body for which his father also sat as member. Like his father, John had fathered children out of wedlock with a common-law wife prior to his marriage.

John Johnson's ascendancy to Fort Johnson coincided with the beginning of the Pontiac Rebellion, the resolution of which his father played a seminal role. The British had won the French and Indian War, and natives, particularly in the Ohio Valley, were reluctant to redirect their allegiances from Louis XVI to King George III. Settler homesteads and forts began to pepper traditional native lands while under British rule. Under the French, whose presence had been less intrusive, the natives had felt less threatened and enjoyed healthy commerce. Other perceived British insults, such as the abandonment of the annual tradition of presenting gifts to tribes and of intermarriage between native women and whites, fueled the uprising.

Sir William Johnson stood alone as a British benefactor to the Indians. Pontiac, an Ottawa chief, led failed raids and sieges of Forts Detroit and Pitt but was successful in attacking eight British forts, including strategic outposts such as Presque Isle and Michilimackinac. Pontiac's men took few prisoners, and thousands of settlers lost their lives and scalps during his raids.

The Proclamation of 1763, a farcical attempt by the British to placate native concerns, failed to slow white settlement west of an imaginary line along the crest of the Appalachian Mountains. Only did the Treaty of Stanwix—negotiated by Sir William—temporarily placate the natives. John Johnson had earned the right to stand by his father's side at Stanwix through his service during the British expeditions into the Ohio Valley in 1764.

John left for Britain for a two-year "grand tour" beginning in 1765. He visited relatives in Ireland and returned in 1767, having received his baronetcy from George III, an indication of the significance the Johnson family held in the royal court. His father continued as a superintendent of Indian affairs until his death in 1774, the same year he negotiated his final treaty, one that ended the blood exchange between the British and the Mingos of the Ohio Valley known as the War of Lord Dunsmore.

Fortunately for John Johnson, he inherited his father's bold disposition in addition to his vast estates. The American Revolution was breaking out early in 1775, with armed conflicts in Lexington and Concord, Massachusetts, and the appointment of George Washington as the commander of the Continental army. In May of that year, John and his cousin Sir Guy Johnson gathered five hundred Tories at Johnson Hall and formally voted to oppose the steps toward independence being taken at the start of the Second Continental Congress in Philadelphia. Guy Johnson had married one of John's stepsisters and had been groomed by Sir William as his replacement as superintendant of Indian affairs. In contrast, John Johnson had been concentrating on the well-being of Loyalists who were on the verge of becoming refugees. He also mustered militia to defy the rebel army.

The pace of the Revolution accelerated during the middle months of 1775, as Americans Benedict Arnold and Ethan Allen took Fort Ticonderoga and the British lost the Battle of Bunker Hill outside of Boston. In response, Guy Johnson began convincing many Iroquois to side with the British. However, Washington's northern general, Philip Schuyler, decided to undercut them both.

Schuyler extended invitations for the native chiefs to parlay with him in Albany, but none of significance came; instead, they went north to Montreal to strategize with the British. Frustrated, he sent three thousand troops to surround John Johnson's home and capture him. Outnumbered ten to one, Johnson and his men laid down their arms and were taken into custody as two other known Loyalists elsewhere in the Mohawk Valley were rounded up.

Schuyler released Johnson "on his honour," but Johnson chose to return to Johnson Hall and offer food and shelter to displaced Loyalists. To his mind, it was the "treasonous" rebels who lacked honor, not him, and he continued to recruit and arm Tory militiamen.

Upon learning this, Congress ordered Schuyler to send another force to recapture Johnson, but this time Johnson escaped just before its arrival. He led 170 of his tenants and Iroquois allies on a two-hundred-mile trek over the Appalachian Mountains to Montreal. In his absence, Johnson Hall and the rest of his property was confiscated.

As it neared the end of the trip, the party luckily fell into the hands of Akwanase natives, who rescued them from starvation and exhaustion. Restored, Johnson reassembled his refugees, added some armed local men and entered Montreal. He discovered that retreating rebel forces were in the area and pursed them in the direction of Fort St. John on the Richelieu River. When he arrived, he encountered Governor Guy Carleton and the new head of the British army, General John Burgoyne.

Sir William Johnson built his Georgian stone home in 1759. He moved a few miles inland to higher ground and a larger estate, Johnson Hall, in 1763. His son John then moved into Fort Johnson (pictured). *Courtesy of Kelly Hunter.*

Gavin Watt and James Morrison described the contrasting appearances of thirty-four-year-old Johnson and fifty-two-year-old Carleton:

> *Sir John Johnson dressed like a frontiersman in…a deerskin jacket and trousers…a scalping knife hung around his throat and in his belt was a tomahawk…Guy Carleton dressed in a scarlet frock coat with gleaming metal buttons, wore a laced cocked hat, and carried a fine sword at his side. An observer would have been hard pressed to recognize that Johnson was the wealthier of the two.*

Though the two men differed in manner, they agreed on the need for a New York regiment, and Carleton ordered Johnson to raise battalions for the King's Royal Regiment of New York. Johnson and Burgoyne pushed the cautious Carleton toward allowing them to attack the Mohawk Valley, but the governor demurred, preferring to prepare for his own assault down Lake Champlain.

The winter of 1776 was a frustrating one for Johnson and his men, as they were ordered to stay in Montreal and work on the local fortifications. Johnson had left his pregnant wife, Polly, and his young son behind at Johnson

GENERAL HER
HOME OF GENERAL NICHOLAS
AT THE BATTLE OF OR

This Mohawk Valley keepsake bears the image of General Nicholas Herkimer's homestead, where he died ten days after the Battle of Oriskany following a botched attempt to amputate his wounded leg. Keepsake scan, 1800s.

Hall when he was forced to escape north. After Polly gave birth, the rebels moved the family from one location to another to discourage any attempts at rescuing them. Eventually, they released her for good behavior and allowed her to stay in Fishkill, New York, but her deportment had been a ruse. She fled south in disguise and was reunited with her husband, who had arrived in New York from Montreal.

OMESTEAD 1764
MMAND OF THE AMERICAN FORCES
WAS MORTALLY WOUNDED.

In June 1777, Johnson finally received the order to attack upstate New York. The target was Fort Stanwix, the site of the modern-day city of Rome and a strategic portage along the Mohawk River that British lieutenant colonel Barry St. Leger had placed under siege. The Tyron County militia, which had once been led by Johnson, was now under General Nicholas Herkimer and traveled west along the Mohawk River to relieve the American fort. As the militiamen camped at the Oneida village of Oriska, Sir John Johnson was dispatched to lead an ambush.

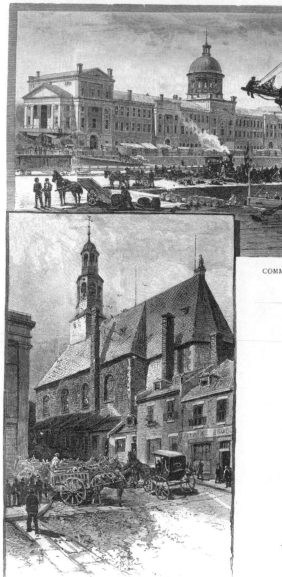

COMMISSIONER'S WHARF, AND BONSECOURS
MARKET.

BONSECOURS CHURCH.

The Bonsecours Market in the heart of Montreal was built on property where Sir John Johnson's mansion once stood. The land originally was the site of the manor of the Baron of Longueuil. Print, 1800s.

Sir John Johnson

With seven hundred of the King's Royals, Indian rangers and Mohawk and Seneca warriors, Johnson took positions around a deep ravine six miles east of the fort. The ambush quickly turned into a pitched battle, in which one-time neighbors fought one another in hand-to-hand combat. When the day ended, Herkimer had been fatally injured and five hundred of his eight hundred men had been killed, captured or wounded. Johnson lost a handful of his Loyalist men, but his native warriors took heavier casualties, retreated prematurely and returned to the fort with their support for the siege eroded. Johnson's victory was Pyrrhic, as St. Leger's siege ended in failure.

Johnson spent the next few years in Montreal and eventually returned to the Mohawk and nearby Schoharie Valleys in 1780. He led a series of ruthless scorched-earth attacks that burned houses, livestock and hundreds of thousands of bushels of grain. His march was devastating and was only halted when he encountered an American force double his size. Wounded, he led his men to a successful retreat and returned to Canada a hero.

After the war, Johnson continued his service to the Crown. In 1782, he was nominated as Indian superintendent and dealt with the tricky task of explaining the implications of the Treaty of Paris to his dispirited and displaced Iroquois allies. He and Polly eventually had a family of eleven children, including eight boys, all of whom served in the British army.

With substantial compensation for his losses in New York, Johnson's wealth returned, and he acquired properties along the north shore of the St. Lawrence River, where he helped hundreds of Loyalist refugees settle. He later sat on the Legislative Council of Lower Canada and was a grand master of the Masonic Order of Quebec. His only major setback came when his name was put forth for lieutenant governor but was disallowed. His vengeful raids in New York State at the end of the war ensured that he would be forever exiled to Canada. He died in Montreal at the age of eighty-eight in 1830, and his funeral was attended by hundreds of Mohawks, just as his father's had been almost sixty years earlier.

Sir John Johnson's tomb on Mount Johnson, present-day Mont-Saint-Grégoire in Quebec's Eastern Townships, lay quietly for more than 120 years until a bulldozer driver unknowingly drove the structure into a pit during the 1950s. The remorse of the man responsible began a chain of events that eventually led to an archaeological survey. The *Brome County News* reported in 2003 that more than eight hundred bones belonging to a handful of adults and children were uncovered. One scattered set of skeletal remains found in the desecrated grave site belonged to an elderly arthritic man and were likely those of Sir John Johnson, the second baronet.

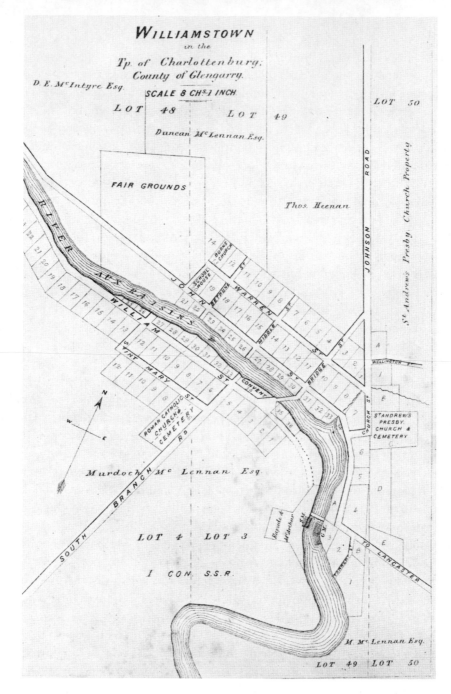

Sir John Johnson owned a home and industrial site in the village of Williamstown, named in honor of his father and situated slightly north of the St. Lawrence River. Despite its size, the hamlet has the most historic plaques of any community in Ontario. Print, 1880s.

Johnson's funeral took place in Christ Church in Montreal, and his body was carried by barge down the St. Lawrence to its final resting place. The Sir John Johnson branch of the United Empire Loyalist Association of Canada is planning a restoration of the Johnson family crypt on Mont-Saint-Grégoire, Quebec. Painting. *Courtesy of the Masonic Grand Lodge of Quebec.*

More than 230 years ago, in Johnstown, New York, another scattered set of family remains was found when the grave site of the first baronet, Sir William Johnson, was desecrated by American rebels, who melted down his coffin for ammunition.

On September 14–15, 2008, the town of Johnstown, New York, celebrated the 250th anniversary of its founding by Sir William. Present were the King's Royal Yorkers, the Loyalist Fifes and Drums and the eighth baronet, Sir Guy Johnson, and his wife, Lady Johnson, from England.

BIBLIOGRAPHY

Shadow Soldiers of the American Revolution is intended for casual readers with an interest in history who are living or traveling in New York, Ontario and Quebec, particularly in the corridors of Lake Champlain, Lake Ontario and the St. Lawrence, Mohawk, Hudson, Richelieu and Rideau Rivers. The titles listed below are a mix of related books published in the United States, Canada and elsewhere. Some address selected geographic regions, while others focus on specific white or native Loyalists or the wider themes of the War of Independence. All are intended for general audiences and students, both juvenile and scholarly.

Beacock Fryer, Mary. *Buckskin Pimpernel: The Exploits of Justus Sherwood, Loyalist Spy.* Toronto: Dundurn Press Ltd., 1995.
———. *King's Men: The Soldier founders of Ontario.* Toronto: Dundurn Press Ltd., 1980.
Blakeley, Phyllis. *Eleven Exiles: Accounts of Loyalists of the American Revolution.* Toronto: Dundurn Press Ltd., 1982.
Earle, Thomas. *The Three Faces of Molly Brant: A Biography.* Kingston, ON: Quarry Press, 1997.
Greene, Jack, and J.R. Pole. *A Companion to the American Revolution.* N.p.: Wiley-Blackwell, 2003.
Lockwood, Glenn J. *Montague: A Social History of an Irish Ontario Township: 1783–1980.* Kingston, ON: Mastercraft Printing and Graphics, 1980.
———. *The Rear of Leeds & Lansdowne: The Making of Community on the Gananoque River Frontier, 1796–1996.* N.p.: Corporation of the Township of Rear of Leeds and Lansdowne, 1996.

————. *Smiths Falls: A Social History of the Men and Women in a Rideau Canal Community, 1794–1994.* Smith Falls, ON: Town of Smiths Falls, 1994.

O'Toole, Fintan. *White Savage: William Johnson & the Invention of America.* London: Faber & Faber, 2005.

Potter-Mackinnon, Janice. *While the Women Only Wept: Loyalist Refugee Women in Eastern Ontario.* Kingston, ON: McGill-Queen's University Press, 1995.

Sheppard, George. *Plunder, Profit and Paroles: A Social History of the War of 1812 in Upper Canada.* Kingston, ON: McGill-Queen's University Press, 1994.

Starkey, Armstrong. *European and Native American warfare, 1675–1815.* Madrid: Editorial Galaxia, 1998.

Thompson Kelsay, Isabel. *Joseph Brant, 1743–1807: Man of Two Worlds.* Syracuse, NY: Syracuse University Press, 1984.

Watt, Gavin K., and James F. Morrison. *The Burning of the Valleys: Daring Raids from Canada against the New York Frontier in the Fall of 1780.* Toronto: Dundurn Press, 1997.

————. *Rebellion in the Mohawk Valley: The St. Leger Expedition of 1777.* Toronto: Dundurn Press, 2002.

ABOUT THE AUTHOR

M ark Jodoin is an author and speaker of subjects related to the history of the American Northeast and Canada. A graduate of Carleton University's School of Journalism, Mr. Jodoin is a former journalist and marketing entrepreneur whose career has taken him across the United States, Canada and Europe. As a heritage writer, his period of interest begins with the U.S. Declaration of Independence in 1776 and continues through to Canada's Confederation in 1867. Mr. Jodoin is the history feature writer for the Canadian magazine *Esprit de Corps* and president of the Rideau Township Historical Society. He lives in Ottawa, Ontario, Canada.

Visit us at
www.historypress.net